HELEN KELLER was born on June 27, 1880, in Tuscumbia, Alabama. At nineteen months old an acute illness nearly took her life and left her deaf and blind. At the recommendation of Alexander Graham Bell, her parents contacted the Perkins Institute for the Blind in Boston, and Anne Sullivan was sent to tutor Helen. The story of their early years together, and of Helen's remarkable psychological and intellectual growth, is told in *The Story of My Life,* which first appeared in installments in *Ladies' Home Journal* in 1902. With Anne Sullivan, "Teacher," at her side, Helen Keller graduated from Radcliffe College in 1904, an extraordinary accomplishment for any woman of her time. Helen was dedicated to helping the blind and handicapped, raising funds for the American Foundation for the Blind and lobbying for commissions for the blind in thirty states. A women's-rights activist, a Swedenborgian, a socialist, and a world-famous celebrity, Helen Keller received the Presidential Medal of Freedom and many honorary degrees. Her other books include *The World I Live In* (1908), *Midstream: My Later Life* (1929), *Helen Keller's Journal* (1938), and *Let Us Have Faith* (1940). She died in 1968. Her burial urn is in the National Cathedral in Washington, D.C.

THE STORY OF MY LIFE

HELEN KELLER

BANTAM CLASSIC

THE STORY OF MY LIFE
A Bantam Book

PUBLISHING HISTORY
Signet edition published October 1988
Bantam Classic edition / June 1990
Bantam Classic reissue / November 2005

Published by
Bantam Dell
A Division of Random House, Inc.
New York, New York

Library of Congress Catalog Card Number: 88-61387

ISBN-13: 978-0-553-21387-4
ISBN-10: 0-553-21387-3

Printed in the United States of America
Published simultaneously in Canada

www.bantamdell.com

OPM   32   31   30   29   28   27   26   25   24

CONTENTS

THE STORY OF MY LIFE

CHAPTER 1

IT IS with a kind of fear that I begin to write the history of my life. I have, as it were, a superstitious hesitation in lifting the veil that clings about my childhood like a golden mist. The task of writing an autobiography is a difficult one. When I try to classify my earliest impressions, I find that fact and fancy look alike across the years that link the past with the present. The woman paints the child's experiences in her own fantasy. A few impressions stand out vividly from the first years of my life; but "the shadows of the prison-house are on the rest." Besides, many of the joys and sorrows of childhood have lost their poignancy; and many incidents of vital importance in my early education have been forgotten in the excitement of great discoveries. In order, therefore, not to be tedious I shall try to present in a series of sketches only the episodes that seem to me to be the most interesting and important.

I was born on June 27, 1880, in Tuscumbia, a little town of northern Alabama.

The family on my father's side is descended from Caspar Keller, a native of Switzerland, who settled in Maryland. One of my Swiss ancestors was the first teacher of the deaf in Zurich and wrote a book on the subject of their education— rather a singular coincidence; though it is true that there is no king who has not had a slave among his ancestors, and no slave who has not had a king among his.

My grandfather, Caspar Keller's son, "entered" large tracts of land in Alabama and finally settled there. I have been told that once a year he went from Tuscumbia to Philadelphia on horseback to purchase supplies for the plantation, and my aunt has in her possession many of the letters to his family, which give charming and vivid accounts of these trips.

My Grandmother Keller was a daughter of one of Lafayette's aides, Alexander Moore, and granddaughter of Alexander Spotswood, an early Colonial Governor of Virginia. She was also second cousin to Robert E. Lee.

My father, Arthur H. Keller, was a captain in the Confederate Army, and my mother, Kate Adams, was his second wife and many years younger. Her grandfather, Benjamin Adams, married Susanna E. Goodhue, and lived in Newbury, Massachusetts, for many years. Their son, Charles Adams, was born in Newburyport, Massachusetts, and moved to Helena, Arkansas. When the Civil War broke out, he fought on the side of the South and became a brigadier-general. He married Lucy Helen Everett, who belonged to the same family of Everetts as Edward Everett and Dr. Edward Everett Hale. After the war was over the family moved to Memphis, Tennessee.

I lived, up to the time of the illness that deprived me of my sight and hearing, in a tiny house consisting of a large square room and a small one, in which the servant slept. It is a custom in the South to build a small house near the homestead as an annex to be used on occasion. Such a house my father built after the Civil War, and when he married my mother they went to live in it. It was completely covered with vines, climbing roses and honeysuckles. From the garden it looked like an arbour. The little porch was hidden from view by a screen of yellow roses and Southern smilax. It was the favourite haunt of hummingbirds and bees.

The Keller homestead, where the family lived, was a few steps from our little rose-bower. It was called "Ivy Green" because the house and the surrounding trees and fences were covered with beautiful English ivy. Its old-fashioned garden was the paradise of my childhood.

Even in the days before my teacher came, I used to feel along the square stiff boxwood hedges, and, guided by the sense of smell, would find the first violets and lilies. There, too, after a fit of temper, I went to find comfort and to hide my hot face in the cool leaves and grass. What joy it was to lose myself in that garden of flowers, to wander happily from spot to spot, until, coming suddenly upon a beautiful vine, I recognized it by its leaves and blossoms, and knew it was the vine which covered the tumble-down summer-house at the farther end of the garden! Here, also, were trailing clematis, drooping jessamine, and some rare sweet flowers called butterfly lilies, because their fragile petals resemble butterflies' wings. But the roses—they were loveliest of all. Never have I found in the greenhouses of the North such heart-satisfying roses as the climbing roses of my southern home. They used to hang in long festoons from our porch, filling the whole air with their fragrance, untainted by any earthy smell; and in the early morning, washed in the dew, they felt so soft, so pure, I could not help wondering if they did not resemble the asphodels of God's garden.

The beginning of my life was simple and much like every other little life. I came, I saw, I conquered, as the first baby in the family always does. There was the usual amount of discussion as to a name for me. The first baby in the family was not to be lightly named, every one was emphatic about that. My father suggested the name of Mildred Campbell, an ancestor whom he highly esteemed, and he declined to take any further part in the discussion. My mother solved the problem by giving it as her wish that I should be called after her mother, whose maiden name was Helen Everett. But in the excitement of carrying me to church my father lost the name on the way, very naturally, since it was one in which he had declined to have a part. When the minister asked him for it, he just remembered that it had been decided to call me after my grandmother, and he gave her name as Helen Adams.

I am told that while I was still in long dresses I showed many signs of an eager, self-asserting disposition. Everything that I saw other people do I insisted upon imitating. At six months I could pipe out "How d'ye," and one day I attracted everyone's attention by saying "Tea, tea, tea" quite plainly.

Even after my illness I remembered one of the words I had learned in these early months. It was the word "water," and I continued to make some sound for that word after all other speech was lost. I ceased making the sound "wah-wah" only when I learned to spell the word.

They tell me I walked the day I was a year old. My mother had just taken me out of the bath-tub and was holding me in her lap, when I was suddenly attracted by the flickering shadows of leaves that danced in the sunlight on the smooth floor. I slipped from my mother's lap and almost ran toward them. The impulse gone, I fell down and cried for her to take me up in her arms.

These happy days did not last long. One brief spring, musical with the song of robin and mockingbird, one summer rich in fruit and roses, one autumn of gold and crimson sped by and left their gifts at the feet of an eager, delighted child. Then, in the dreary month of February, came the illness which closed my eyes and ears and plunged me into the unconsciousness of a newborn baby. They called it acute congestion of the stomach and brain. The doctor thought I could not live. Early one morning, however, the fever left me as suddenly and mysteriously as it had come. There was great rejoicing in the family that morning, but no one, not even the doctor, knew that I should never see or hear again.

I fancy I still have confused recollections of that illness. I especially remember the tenderness with which my mother tried to soothe me in my waking hours of fret and pain, and the agony and bewilderment with which I awoke after a tossing half sleep, and turned my eyes, so dry and hot, to the wall, away from the once-loved light, which came to me dim and yet more dim each day. But, except for these fleeting memories, if, indeed, they be memories, it all seems very unreal, like a nightmare. Gradually I got used to the silence and darkness that surrounded me and forgot that it had ever been different, until she came—my teacher—who was to set my spirit free. But during the first nineteen months of my life I had caught glimpses of broad, green fields, a luminous sky, trees and flowers which the darkness that followed could not wholly blot out. If we have once seen, "the day is ours, and what the day has shown."

CHAPTER 2

I CANNOT RECALL what happened during the first months after my illness. I only know that I sat in my mother's lap or clung to her dress as she went about her household duties. My hands felt every object and observed every motion, and in this way I learned to know many things. Soon I felt the need of some communication with others and began to make crude signs. A shake of the head meant "No" and a nod, "Yes," a pull meant "Come" and a push "Go." Was it bread that I wanted? Then I would imitate the acts of cutting the slices and buttering them. If I wanted my mother to make ice-cream for dinner I made the sign for working the freezer and shivered, indicating cold. My mother, moreover, succeeded in making me understand a good deal. I always knew when she wished me to bring her something, and I would run upstairs or anywhere else she indicated. Indeed, I owe to her loving wisdom all that was bright and good in my long night.

I understood a good deal of what was going on about me. At five I learned to fold and put away the clean clothes when they were brought in from the laundry, and I distinguished my own from the rest. I knew by the way my mother and aunt dressed when they were going out, and I invariably begged to go with them. I was always sent for when there was company, and when the guests took their leave, I waved my hand to them, I think with a vague remembrance of the meaning of the gesture. One day some gentlemen called on my mother, and I felt the shutting of the front door and other sounds that indicated their arrival. On a sudden thought I ran upstairs before any one could stop me, to put on my idea of a company dress. Standing before the mirror, as I had seen others do, I annointed mine head with oil and covered my face thickly with powder. Then I pinned a veil over my head so that it covered my face and fell in folds down to my shoulders, and tied an enormous bustle round my small waist, so that it dangled behind, almost meeting the hem of my skirt. Thus attired I went down to help entertain the company.

I do not remember when I first realized that I was different from other people; but I knew it before my teacher came to me. I had noticed that my mother and my friends did not use signs as I did when they wanted anything done, but talked with their mouths. Sometimes I stood between two persons who were conversing and touched their lips. I could not understand, and was vexed. I moved my lips and gesticulated frantically without result. This made me so angry at times that I kicked and screamed until I was exhausted.

I think I knew when I was naughty, for I knew that it hurt Ella, my nurse, to kick her, and when my fit of temper was over I had a feeling akin to regret. But I cannot remember any instance in which this feeling prevented me from repeating the naughtiness when I failed to get what I wanted.

In those days a little coloured girl, Martha Washington, the child of our cook, and Belle, an old setter and a great hunter in her day, were my constant companions. Martha Washington understood my signs, and I seldom had any difficulty in making her do just as I wished. It pleased me to domineer over her, and she generally submitted to my tyranny rather than risk a hand-to-hand encounter. I was strong, active, indifferent to consequences. I knew my own mind well enough and always had my own way, even if I had to fight tooth and nail for it. We spent a great deal of time in the kitchen, kneading dough balls, helping make ice-cream, grinding coffee, quarreling over the cake-bowl, and feeding the hens and turkeys that swarmed about the kitchen steps.

Many of them were so tame that they would eat from my hand and let me feel them. One big gobbler snatched a tomato from me one day and ran away with it. Inspired, perhaps, by Master Gobbler's success, we carried off to the woodpile a cake which the cook had just frosted, and ate every bit of it. I was quite ill afterward, and I wonder if retribution also overtook the turkey.

The guinea-fowl likes to hide her nest in out-of-the-way places, and it was one of my greatest delights to hunt for the eggs in the long grass. I could not tell Martha Washington when I wanted to go egg-hunting, but I would double my hands and put them on the ground, which meant something round in the grass, and Martha always understood. When we were fortunate enough to find a nest I never allowed her to carry the eggs home, making her understand by emphatic signs that she might fall and break them.

The sheds where the corn was stored, the stable where the horses were kept, and the yard where the cows were milked morning and evening were unfailing sources of interest to Martha and me. The milkers would let me keep my hands on the cows while they milked, and I often got well switched by the cows for my curiosity.

The making ready for Christmas was always a delight to me. Of course I did not know what it was all about, but I enjoyed the pleasant odours that filled the house and the tidbits that were given to Martha Washington and me to keep us quiet. We were sadly in the way, but that did not interfere with our pleasure in the least. They allowed us to grind the spices, pick over the raisins and lick the stirring spoons. I hung my stocking because the others did; I cannot remember, however, that the ceremony interested me especially, nor did my curiosity cause me to wake before daylight to look for my gifts.

Martha Washington had as great a love of mischief as I. Two little children were seated on the veranda steps one hot July afternoon. One was black as ebony, with little bunches of fuzzy hair tied with shoestrings sticking out all over her head like corkscrews. The other was white, with long golden curls.

One child was six years old, the other two or three years older. The younger child was blind—that was I—and the other was Martha Washington. We were busy cutting out paper dolls; but we soon wearied of this amusement, and after cutting up our shoestrings and clipping all the leaves off the honeysuckle that were within reach, I turned my attention to Martha's corkscrews. She objected at first, but finally submitted. Thinking that turn and turn about is fair play, she seized the scissors and cut off one of my curls, and would have cut them all off but for my mother's timely interference.

Belle, our dog, my other companion, was old and lazy and liked to sleep by the open fire rather than to romp with me. I tried hard to teach her my sign language, but she was dull and inattentive. She sometimes started and quivered with excitement, then she became perfectly rigid, as dogs do when they point a bird. I did not then know why Belle acted in this way; but I knew she was not doing as I wished. This vexed me and the lesson always ended in a one-sided boxing match. Belle would get up, stretch herself lazily, give one or two contemptuous sniffs, go to the opposite side of the hearth and lie down again, and I, wearied and disappointed, went off in search of Martha.

Many incidents of those early years are fixed in my memory, isolated, but clear and distinct, making the sense of that silent, aimless, dayless life all the more intense.

One day I happened to spill water on my apron, and I spread it out to dry before the fire which was flickering on the sitting-room hearth. The apron did not dry quickly enough to suit me, so I drew nearer and threw it right over the hot ashes. The fire leaped into life; the flames encircled me so that in a moment my clothes were blazing. I made a terrified noise that brought Viny, my old nurse, to the rescue. Throwing a blanket over me, she almost suffocated me, but she put out the fire. Except for my hands and hair I was not badly burned.

About this time I found out the use of a key. One morning I locked my mother up in the pantry, where she was obliged to remain three hours, as the servants were in a detached part of the house. She kept pounding on the door, while I sat outside on the porch steps and laughed with glee as I felt the jar of the pounding. This most naughty prank of mine convinced my parents that I must be taught as soon as possible. After my teacher, Miss Sullivan, came to me, I sought an early opportunity to lock her in her room. I went upstairs with something which my mother made me understand I was to give to Miss Sullivan; but no sooner had I given it to her than I slammed the door to, locked it, and hid the key under the wardrobe in the hall. I could not be induced to tell where the key was. My father was obliged to get a ladder and take Miss Sullivan out through the window—much to my delight. Months after I produced the key.

When I was about five years old we moved from the little vine-covered house to a large new one. The family consisted of my father and mother, two older half-brothers, and, afterward, a little sister, Mildred. My earliest distinct recollection of my father is making my way through great drifts of newspapers to his side and finding him alone, holding a sheet of paper before his face. I was greatly puzzled to know what he was doing. I imitated this action, even wearing his spectacles, thinking they might help solve the mystery. But I did not find out the secret for several years. Then I learned what those papers were, and that my father edited one of them.

My father was most loving and indulgent, devoted to his home, seldom leaving us, except in the hunting season. He was a great hunter, I have been told, and a celebrated shot. Next to his family he loved his dogs and gun. His hospitality was great, almost to a fault, and he seldom came home without bringing a guest. His special pride was the big garden where, it was said, he raised the finest watermelons and strawberries in the country; and to me he brought the first ripe grapes and the choicest berries. I remember his caressing touch as he led me from tree to tree, from vine to vine, and his eager delight in whatever pleased me.

He was a famous story-teller; after I had acquired language he used to spell clumsily into my hand his cleverest

anecdotes, and nothing pleased him more than to have me repeat them at an opportune moment.

I was in the North, enjoying the last beautiful days of the
summer of 1896, when I heard the news of my father's death.
He had had a short illness, there had been a brief time of
acute suffering, then all was over. This was my first great sorrow—my first personal experience with death.

How shall I write of my mother? She is so near to me that
it almost seems indelicate to speak of her.

For a long time I regarded my little sister as an intruder. I
knew that I had ceased to be my mother's only darling, and
the thought filled me with jealousy. She sat in my mother's
lap constantly, where I used to sit, and seemed to take up all
her care and time. One day something happened which
seemed to me to be adding insult to injury.

At that time I had a much-petted, much-abused doll, which
I afterward named Nancy. She was, alas, the helpless victim
of my outbursts of temper and of affection, so that she became much the worse for wear. I had dolls which talked, and
cried, and opened and shut their eyes; yet I never loved one of
them as I loved poor Nancy. She had a cradle, and I often
spent an hour or more rocking her. I guarded both doll and
cradle with the most jealous care; but once I discovered my
little sister sleeping peacefully in the cradle. At this presump-
tion on the part of one to whom as yet no tie of love bound me
I grew angry. I rushed upon the cradle and overturned it, and
the baby might have been killed had my mother not caught
her as she fell. Thus it is that when we walk in the valley of
twofold solitude we know little of the tender affections that
grow out of endearing words and actions and companionship.
But afterward, when I was restored to my human heritage,
Mildred and I grew into each other's hearts, so that we were
content to go hand-in-hand wherever caprice led us, although
she could not understand my finger language, nor I her childish prattle.

CHAPTER 3

MEANWHILE, THE desire to express myself grew. The few signs I used became less and less adequate, and my failures to make myself understood were invariably followed by outbursts of passion. I felt as if invisible hands were holding me, and I made frantic efforts to free myself. I struggled—not that struggling helped matters, but the spirit of resistance was strong within me; I generally broke down in tears and physical exhaustion. If my mother happened to be near I crept into her arms, too miserable even to remember the cause of the tempest. After awhile the need of some means of communication became so urgent that these outbursts occurred daily, sometimes hourly.

My parents were deeply grieved and perplexed. We lived a long way from any school for the blind or the deaf, and it seemed unlikely that any one would come to such an out-of-the-way place as Tuscumbia to teach a child who was both deaf and blind. Indeed, my friends and relatives sometimes doubted whether I could be taught. My mother's only ray of hope came from Dickens's "American Notes." She had read his account of Laura Bridgman, and remembered vaguely that she was deaf and blind, yet had been educated. But she also remembered with a hopeless pang that Dr. Howe, who had discovered the way to teach the deaf and blind, had been dead many years. His methods had probably died with him; and if they had not, how was a little girl in a far-off town in Alabama to receive the benefit of them?

When I was about six years old, my father heard of an eminent oculist in Baltimore, who had been successful in many cases that had seemed hopeless. My parents at once determined to take me to Baltimore to see if anything could be done for my eyes.

The journey, which I remember well, was very pleasant. I made friends with many people on the train. One lady gave me a box of shells. My father made holes in these so that I could string them, and for a long time they kept me happy and contented. The conductor, too, was kind. Often when he went his rounds I clung to his coat tails while he collected and punched the tickets. His punch, with which he let me play, was a delightful toy. Curled up in a corner of the seat I amused myself for hours making funny little holes in bits of cardboard.

My aunt made me a big doll out of towels. It was the most comical, shapeless thing, this improvised doll, with no nose, mouth, ears or eyes—nothing that even the imagination of a child could convert into a face. Curiously enough, the absence of eyes struck me more than all the other defects put together. I pointed this out to everybody with provoking persistency, but no one seemed equal to the task of providing the doll with eyes. A bright idea, however, shot into my mind, and the problem was solved. I tumbled off the seat and searched under it until I found my aunt's cape, which was trimmed with large beads. I pulled two beads off and indicated to her that I wanted her to sew them on my doll. She raised my hand to her eyes in a questioning way, and I nodded energetically. The beads were sewed in the right place and I could not contain myself for joy; but immediately I lost all interest in the doll. During the whole trip I did not have one fit of temper, there were so many things to keep my mind and fingers busy.

When we arrived in Baltimore, Dr. Chisholm received us kindly: but he could do nothing. He said, however, that I could be educated, and advised my father to consult Dr. Alexander Graham Bell, of Washington, who would be able to give him information about schools and teachers of deaf or blind children. Acting on the doctor's advice, we went immediately to Washington to see Dr. Bell, my father with a sad heart and many misgivings, I wholly unconscious of his anguish, finding pleasure in the excitement of moving from place to place. Child as I was, I at once felt the tenderness and sympathy which endeared Dr. Bell to so many hearts, as his wonderful achievements enlist their admiration. He held me on his knee while I examined his watch, and he made it strike for me. He understood my signs, and I knew it and loved him at once. But I did not dream that that interview would be the door through which I should pass from darkness into light, from isolation to friendship, companionship, knowledge, love.

Dr. Bell advised my father to write to Mr. Anagnos, director of the Perkins Institution in Boston, the scene of Dr. Howe's great labours for the blind, and ask him if he had a teacher competent to begin my education. This my father did at once, and in a few weeks there came a kind letter from Mr. Anagnos with the comforting assurance that a teacher had been found. This was in the summer of 1886. But Miss Sullivan did not arrive until the following March.

Thus I came up out of Egypt and stood before Sinai, and a power divine touched my spirit and gave it sight, so that I beheld many wonders. And from the sacred mountain I heard a voice which said, "Knowledge is love and light and vision."

CHAPTER 4

THE MOST important day I remember in all my life is the one on which my teacher, Anne Mansfield Sullivan, came to me. I am filled with wonder when I consider the immeasurable contrasts between the two lives which it connects. It was the third of March, 1887, three months before I was seven years old.

On the afternoon of that eventful day, I stood on the porch, dumb, expectant. I guessed vaguely from my mother's signs and from the hurrying to and fro in the house that something unusual was about to happen, so I went to the door and waited on the steps. The afternoon sun penetrated the mass of honeysuckle that covered the porch, and fell on my upturned face. My fingers lingered almost unconsciously on the familiar leaves and blossoms which had just come forth to greet the sweet southern spring. I did not know what the future held of marvel or surprise for me. Anger and bitterness had preyed upon me continually for weeks and a deep languor had succeeded this passionate struggle.

Have you ever been at sea in a dense fog, when it seemed as if a tangible white darkness shut you in, and the great ship, tense and anxious, groped her way toward the shore with plummet and sounding-line, and you waited with beating heart for something to happen? I was like that ship before my education began, only I was without compass or sounding-line, and had no way of knowing how near the harbour was. "Light! give me light!" was the wordless cry of my soul, and the light of love shone on me in that very hour.

I felt approaching footsteps. I stretched out my hand as I supposed to my mother. Some one took it, and I was caught up and held close in the arms of her who had come to reveal all things to me, and, more than all things else, to love me.

The morning after my teacher came she led me into her room and gave me a doll. The little blind children at the Perkins Institution had sent it and Laura Bridgman had dressed it; but I did not know this until afterward. When I had played with it a little while, Miss Sullivan slowly spelled into my hand the word "d-o-l-l." I was at once interested in this finger play and tried to imitate it. When I finally succeeded in making the letters correctly I was flushed with childish pleasure and pride. Running downstairs to my mother I held up my hand and made the letters for doll. I did not know that I was spelling a word or even that words existed; I was simply making my fingers go in monkey-like imitation. In the days that followed I learned to spell in this uncomprehending way a great many words, among them *pin, hat, cup* and a few verbs like *sit, stand* and *walk*. But my teacher had been with me several weeks before I understood that everything has a name.

One day, while I was playing with my new doll, Miss Sullivan put my big rag doll into my lap also, spelled, "d-o-l-l" and tried to make me understand that "d-o-l-l" applied to both. Earlier in the day we had had a tussle over the words "m-u-g" and "w-a-t-e-r." Miss Sullivan had tried to impress upon me that "m-u-g" is *mug* and that "w-a-t-e-r" is *water*, but I persisted in confounding the two. In despair she had dropped the subject for the time, only to renew it at the first opportunity. I became impatient at her repeated attempts and, seizing the new doll, I dashed it upon the floor. I was keenly delighted when I felt the fragments of the broken doll at my feet. Neither sorrow nor regret followed my passionate outburst. I had not loved the doll. In the still, dark world in which I lived there was no strong sentiment or tenderness. I felt my teacher sweep the fragments to one side of the hearth and I had a sense of satisfaction that the cause of my discomfort was removed. She brought me my hat, and I knew I was going out into the warm sunshine. This thought, if a wordless sensation may be called a thought, made me hop and skip with pleasure.

We walked down the path to the well-house, attracted by the fragrance of the honeysuckle with which it was covered. Someone was drawing water and my teacher placed my hand under the spout. As the cool stream gushed over one hand she spelled into the other the word *water,* first slowly, then rapidly. I stood still, my whole attention fixed upon the motions of her fingers. Suddenly I felt a misty consciousness as of something forgotten—a thrill of returning thought; and somehow the mystery of language was revealed to me. I knew then that "w-a-t-e-r" meant the wonderful cool something that was flowing over my hand. That living word awakened my soul, gave it light, hope, joy, set it free! There were barriers still, it is true, but barriers that could in time be swept away.

I left the well-house eager to learn. Everything had a name, and each name gave birth to a new thought. As we returned to the house every object which I touched seemed to quiver with life. That was because I saw everything with the strange, new sight that had come to me. On entering the door I remembered the doll I had broken. I felt my way to the hearth and picked up the pieces. I tried vainly to put them together. Then my eyes filled with tears; for I realized what I had done, and for the first time I felt repentance and sorrow.

I learned a great many new words that day. I do not remember what they all were; but I do know that *mother, father, sister, teacher* were among them—words that were to make the world blossom for me, "like Aaron's rod, with flowers." It would have been difficult to find a happier child than I was as I lay in my crib at the close of that eventful day and lived over the joys it had brought me, and for the first time longed for a new day to come.

CHAPTER 5

I RECALL MANY incidents of the summer of 1887 that followed my soul's sudden awakening. I did nothing but explore with my hands and learn the name of every object that I touched; and the more I handled things and learned their names and uses, the more joyous and confident grew my sense of kinship with the rest of the world.

When the time of daisies and buttercups came Miss Sullivan took me by the hand across the fields, where men were preparing the earth for the seed, to the banks of the Tennessee River, and there, sitting on the warm grass, I had my first lesson in the beneficence of nature. I learned how the sun and the rain make to grow out of the ground every tree that is pleasant to the sight and good for food, how birds build their nests and live and thrive from land to land, how the squirrel, the deer, the lion and every other creature finds food and shelter. As my knowledge of things grew I felt more and more the delight of the world I was in. Long before I learned to do a sum in arithmetic or describe the shape of the earth, Miss Sullivan had taught me to find beauty in the fragrant woods, in every blade of grass, and in the curves and dimples of my baby sister's hand. She linked my earliest thoughts with nature, and made me feel that "birds and flowers and I were happy peers."

But about this time I had an experience which taught me that nature is not always kind. One day my teacher and I were returning from a long ramble. The morning had been fine, but it was growing warm and sultry when at last we turned our faces homeward. Two or three times we stopped to rest under a tree by the wayside. Our last halt was under a wild cherry tree a short distance from the house. The shade was grateful, and the tree was so easy to climb that with my teacher's assistance I was able to scramble to a seat in the branches. It was so cool up in the tree that Miss Sullivan proposed that we have our luncheon there. I promised to keep still while she went to the house to fetch it.

Suddenly a change passed over the tree. All the sun's warmth left the air. I knew the sky was black, because all the heat, which meant light to me, had died out of the atmosphere. A strange odour came up from the earth. I knew it, it was the odour that always precedes a thunderstorm, and a nameless fear clutched at my heart. I felt absolutely alone, cut off from my friends and the firm earth. The immense, the unknown, enfolded me. I remained still and expectant; a chilling terror crept over me. I longed for my teacher's return; but above all things I wanted to get down from that tree.

There was a moment of sinister silence, then a multitudinous stirring of the leaves. A shiver ran through the tree, and the wind sent forth a blast that would have knocked me off had I not clung to the branch with might and main. The tree swayed and strained. The small twigs snapped and fell about me in showers. A wild impulse to jump seized me, but terror held me fast. I crouched down in the fork of the tree. The branches lashed about me. I felt the intermittent jarring that came now and then, as if something heavy had fallen and the shock had traveled up till it reached the limb I sat on. It worked my suspense up to the highest point, and just as I was thinking the tree and I should fall together, my teacher seized my hand and helped me down. I clung to her, trembling with joy to feel the earth under my feet once more. I had learned a new lesson—that nature "wages open war against her children, and under softest touch hides treacherous claws."

After this experience it was a long time before I climbed another tree. The mere thought filled me with terror. It was the sweet allurement of the mimosa tree in full bloom that finally overcame my fears. One beautiful spring morning when I was alone in the summer-house, reading, I became aware of a wonderful subtle fragrance in the air. I started up and instinctively stretched out my hands. It seemed as if the spirit of spring had passed through the summer-house. "What is it?" I asked, and the next minute I recognized the odour of the mimosa blossoms. I felt my way to the end of the garden, knowing that the mimosa tree was near the fence, at the turn of the path. Yes, there it was, all quivering in the warm sunshine, its blossom-laden branches almost touching the long grass. Was there ever anything so exquisitely beautiful in the world before! Its delicate blossoms shrank from the slightest earthly touch; it seemed as if a tree of paradise had been transplanted to earth. I made my way through a shower of petals to the great trunk and for one minute stood irresolute; then, putting my foot in the broad space between the forked branches, I pulled myself up into the tree. I had some difficulty in holding on, for the branches were very large and the bark hurt my hands. But I had a delicious sense that I was doing something unusual and wonderful, so I kept on climbing higher and higher, until I reached a little seat which somebody had built there so long ago that it had grown part of the tree itself. I sat there for a long, long time, feeling like a fairy on a rosy cloud. After that I spent many happy hours in my tree of paradise, thinking fair thoughts and dreaming bright dreams.

CHAPTER 6

I HAD NOW the key to all language, and I was eager to learn to use it. Children who hear acquire language without any particular effort; the words that fall from others' lips they catch on the wing, as it were, delightedly, while the little deaf child must trap them by a slow and often painful process. But whatever the process, the result is wonderful. Gradually from naming an object we advance step by step until we have traversed the vast distance between our first stammered syllable and the sweep of thought in a line of Shakespeare.

At first, when my teacher told me about a new thing I asked very few questions. My ideas were vague, and my vocabulary was inadequate; but as my knowledge of things grew, and I learned more and more words, my field of inquiry broadened, and I would return again and again to the same subject, eager for further information. Sometimes a new word revived an image that some earlier experience had engraved on my brain.

I remember the morning that I first asked the meaning of the word "love." This was before I knew many words. I had found a few early violets in the garden and brought them to my teacher. She tried to kiss me; but at that time I did not like to have any one kiss me except my mother. Miss Sullivan put her arm gently round me and spelled into my hand, "I love Helen."

"What is love?" I asked.

She drew me closer to her and said, "It is here," pointing to my heart, whose beats I was conscious of for the first time. Her words puzzled me very much because I did not then understand anything unless I touched it.

I smelt the violets in her hand and asked, half in words, half in signs, a question which meant, "Is love the sweetness of flowers?"

"No," said my teacher.

Again I thought. The warm sun was shining on us.

"Is this not love?" I asked, pointing in the direction from which the heat came, "Is this not love?"

It seemed to me that there could be nothing more beautiful than the sun, whose warmth makes all things grow. But Miss Sullivan shook her head, and I was greatly puzzled and disappointed. I thought it strange that my teacher could not show me love.

A day or two afterward I was stringing beads of different sizes in symmetrical groups—two large beads, three small ones, and so on. I had made many mistakes, and Miss Sullivan had pointed them out again and again with gentle patience. Finally I noticed a very obvious error in the sequence and for an instant I concentrated my attention on the lesson and tried to think how I should have arranged the beads. Miss Sullivan touched my forehead and spelled with decided emphasis, "Think."

In a flash I knew that the word was the name of the process that was going on in my head. This was my first conscious perception of an abstract idea.

For a long time I was still—I was not thinking of the beads in my lap, but trying to find a meaning for "love" in the light of this new idea. The sun had been under a cloud all day, and there had been brief showers; but suddenly the sun broke forth in all its southern splendour.

Again I asked my teacher, "Is this not love?"

"Love is something like the clouds that were in the sky before the sun came out," she replied. Then in simpler words than these, which at that time I could not have understood, she explained: "You cannot touch the clouds, you know; but you feel the rain and know how glad the flowers and the thirsty earth are to have it after a hot day. You cannot touch love either; but you feel the sweetness that it pours into everything. Without love you would not be happy or want to play."

The beautiful truth burst upon my mind—I felt that there were invisible lines stretched between my spirit and the spirits of others.

From the beginning of my education Miss Sullivan made it a practice to speak to me as she would speak to any hearing child; the only difference was that she spelled the sentences into my hand instead of speaking them. If I did not know the words and idioms necessary to express my thoughts she supplied them, even suggesting conversation when I was unable to keep up my end of the dialogue.

This process was continued for several years; for the deaf child does not learn in a month, or even in two or three years, the numberless idioms and expressions used in the simplest daily intercourse. The little hearing child learns these from constant repetition and imitation. The conversation he hears in his home stimulates his mind and suggests topics and calls forth the spontaneous expression of his own thoughts. This natural exchange of ideas is denied to the deaf child. My teacher, realizing this, determined to supply the kinds of stimuli I lacked. This she did by repeating to me as far as possible, verbatim, what she heard, and by showing me how I could take part in the conversation. But it was a long time before I ventured to take the initiative, and still longer before I could find something appropriate to say at the right time.

The deaf and the blind find it very difficult to acquire the amenities of conversation. How much more this difficulty must be augmented in the case of those who are both deaf and blind! They cannot distinguish the tone of the voice or, without assistance, go up and down the gamut of tones that give significance to words; nor can they watch the expression of the speaker's face, and a look is often the very soul of what one says.

CHAPTER 7

T HE NEXT important step in my education was learning
to read.

As soon as I could spell a few words my teacher gave me
slips of cardboard on which were printed words in raised letters. I quickly learned that each printed word stood for an object, an act, or a quality. I had a frame in which I could
arrange the words in little sentences; but before I ever put
sentences in the frame I used to make them in objects. I found
the slips of paper which represented, for example, "doll,"
"is," "on," "bed" and placed each name on its object; then I
put my doll on the bed with the words *is, on, bed* arranged beside the doll, thus making a sentence of the words, and at the
same time carrying out the idea of the sentence with the
things themselves.

One day, Miss Sullivan tells me, I pinned the word *girl* on
my pinafore and stood in the wardrobe. On the shelf I arranged the words, *is, in, wardrobe*. Nothing delighted me so
much as this game. My teacher and I played it for hours at a
time. Often everything in the room was arranged in object
sentences.

From the printed slip it was but a step to the printed book.
I took my "Reader for Beginners" and hunted for the words I
knew; when I found them my joy was like that of a game of
hide-and-seek. Thus I began to read. Of the time when I began to read connected stories I shall speak later.

For a long time I had no regular lessons. Even when I studied most earnestly it seemed more like play than work.
Everything Miss Sullivan taught me she illustrated by a beautiful story or a poem. Whenever anything delighted or inter-

ested me she talked it over with me just as if she were a little girl herself. What many children think of with dread, as a painful plodding through grammar, hard sums and harder definitions, is to-day one of my most precious memories.

I cannot explain the peculiar sympathy Miss Sullivan had with my pleasures and desires. Perhaps it was the result of long association with the blind. Added to this she had a wonderful faculty for description. She went quickly over uninteresting details, and never nagged me with questions to see if I remembered the day-before-yesterday's lesson. She introduced dry technicalities of science little by little, making every subject so real that I could not help remembering what she taught.

We read and studied out of doors, preferring the sunlit woods to the house. All my early lessons have in them the breath of the woods—the fine, resinous odour of pine needles, blended with the perfume of wild grapes. Seated in the gracious shade of a wild tulip tree, I learned to think that everything has a lesson and a suggestion. "The loveliness of things taught me all their use." Indeed, everything that could hum, or buzz, or sing, or bloom, had a part in my education— noisy-throated frogs, katydids and crickets held in my hand until, forgetting their embarrassment, they trilled their reedy note, little downy chickens and wildflowers, the dogwood blossoms, meadow-violets and budding fruit trees. I felt the bursting cotton-bolls and fingered their soft fiber and fuzzy seeds; I felt the low soughing of the wind through the cornstalks, the silky rustling of the long leaves, and the indignant snort of my pony, as we caught him in the pasture and put the bit in his mouth—ah me! how well I remember the spicy, clovery smell of his breath!

Sometimes I rose at dawn and stole into the garden while the heavy dew lay on the grass and flowers. Few know what joy it is to feel the roses pressing softly into the hand, or the beautiful motion of the lilies as they sway in the morning breeze. Sometimes I caught an insect in the flower I was plucking, and I felt the faint noise of a pair of wings rubbed together in a sudden terror, as the little creature became aware of a pressure from without.

Another favourite haunt of mine was the orchard, where the fruit ripened early in July. The large, downy peaches would reach themselves into my hand, and as the joyous breezes flew about the trees the apples tumbled at my feet. Oh, the delight with which I gathered up the fruit in my pinafore, pressed my face against the smooth cheeks of the apples, still warm from the sun, and skipped back to the house!

Our favourite walk was to Keller's Landing, an old tumble-down lumber-wharf on the Tennessee River, used during the Civil War to land soldiers. There we spent many happy hours and played at learning geography. I built dams of pebbles, made islands and lakes, and dug river-beds, all for fun, and never dreamed that I was learning a lesson. I listened with increasing wonder to Miss Sullivan's descriptions of the great round world with its burning mountains, buried cities, moving rivers of ice, and many other things as strange. She made raised maps in clay, so that I could feel the mountain ridges and valleys, and follow with my fingers the devious course of rivers. I liked this, too; but the division of the earth into zones and poles confused and teased my mind. The illustrative strings and the orange sticks representing the poles seemed so real that even to this day the mere mention of temperature zone suggests a series of twine circles; and I believe that if any one should set about it he could convince me that white bears actually climb the North Pole.

Arithmetic seems to have been the only study I did not like. From the first I was not interested in the science of numbers. Miss Sullivan tried to teach me to count by stringing beads in groups, and by arranging kindergarten straws I learned to add and subtract. I never had patience to arrange more than five or six groups at a time. When I had accomplished this my conscience was at rest for the day, and I went out quickly to find my playmates.

In the same leisurely manner I studied zoölogy and botany.

Once a gentleman, whose name I have forgotten, sent me a collection of fossils—tiny mollusk shells beautifully marked, and bits of sandstone with the print of birds' claws, and a lovely fern in bas-relief. These were the keys which unlocked the treasures of the antediluvian world for me. With trembling fingers I listened to Miss Sullivan's descriptions of the terrible beasts with uncouth, unpronounceable names, which once went tramping through the primeval forests, tearing down the branches of gigantic trees for food, and died in the dismal swamps of an unknown age. For a long time these strange creatures haunted my dreams, and this gloomy period formed a somber background to the joyous Now, filled with sunshine and roses and echoing with the gentle beat of my pony's hoof.

Another time a beautiful shell was given me, and with a child's surprise and delight I learned how a tiny mollusk had built the lustrous coil for his dwelling place, and how on still nights, when there is no breeze stirring the waves, the Nautilus sails on the blue waters of the Indian Ocean in his "ship of pearl." After I had learned a great many interesting things about the life and habits of the children of the sea—how in the midst of dashing waves the little polyps build the beautiful coral isles of the Pacific, and the foraminifera have made the chalkhills of many a land—my teacher read me "The Chambered Nautilus," and showed me that the shell-building process of the mollusks is symbolical of the development of the mind. Just as the wonder-working mantle of the Nautilus changes the material it absorbs from the water and makes it a part of itself, so the bits of knowledge one gathers undergo a similar change and become pearls of thought.

Again, it was the growth of a plant that furnished the text for a lesson. We bought a lily and set it in a sunny window. Very soon the green, pointed buds showed signs of opening. The slender, fingerlike leaves on the outside opened slowly, reluctant, I thought, to reveal the loveliness they hid; once having made a start, however, the opening process went on rapidly, but in order and systematically. There was always one bud larger and more beautiful than the rest, which pushed her outer covering back with more pomp, as if the beauty in soft, silky robes knew that she was the lily-queen by right divine, while her more timid sisters doffed their green hoods shyly, until the whole plant was one nodding bough of loveliness and fragrance.

Once there were eleven tadpoles in a glass globe set in a window full of plants. I remember the eagerness with which I made discoveries about them. It was great fun to plunge my hand into the bowl and feel the tadpoles frisk about, and to let them slip and slide between my fingers. One day a more ambitious fellow leaped beyond the edge of the bowl and fell on the floor, where I found him to all appearance more dead than alive. The only sign of life was a slight wriggling of his tail. But no sooner had he returned to his element than he darted to the bottom, swimming round and round in joyous activity. He had made his leap, he had seen the great world, and was content to stay in his pretty glass house under the big fuchsia tree until he attained the dignity of froghood. Then he went to live in the leafy pool at the end of the garden, where he made the summer nights musical with his quaint love-song.

Thus I learned from life itself. At the beginning I was only a little mass of possibilities. It was my teacher who unfolded and developed them. When she came, everything about me breathed of love and joy and was full of meaning. She has never since let pass an opportunity to point out the beauty that is in everything, nor has she ceased trying in thought and action and example to make my life sweet and useful.

It was my teacher's genius, her quick sympathy, her loving tact which made the first years of my education so beautiful. It was because she seized the right moment to impart knowledge that made it so pleasant and acceptable to me. She realized that a child's mind is like a shallow brook which ripples and dances merrily over the stony course of its education and reflects here a flower, there a bush, yonder a fleecy cloud; and she attempted to guide my mind on its way, knowing that like a brook it should be fed by mountain streams and hidden springs, until it broadened out into a deep river, capable of reflecting in its placid surface, billowy hills, the luminous shadows of trees and the blue heavens, as well as the sweet face of a little flower.

Any teacher can take a child to the classroom, but not every teacher can make him learn. He will not work joyously unless he feels that liberty is his, whether he is busy or at rest; he must feel the flush of victory and the heart-sinking of disappointment before he takes with a will the tasks distasteful to him and resolves to dance his way bravely through a dull routine of textbooks.

My teacher is so near to me that I scarcely think of myself apart from her. How much of my delight in all beautiful things is innate, and how much is due to her influence, I can never tell. I feel that her being is inseparable from my own, and that the footsteps of my life are in hers. All the best of me belongs to her—there is not a talent, or an inspiration or a joy in me that has not awakened by her loving touch.

CHAPTER 8

THE FIRST Christmas after Miss Sullivan came to Tuscumbia was a great event. Every one in the family prepared surprises for me, but what pleased me most, Miss Sullivan and I prepared surprises for everybody else. The mystery that surrounded the gifts was my greatest delight and amusement. My friends did all they could to excite my curiosity by hints and half-spelled sentences which they pretended to break off in the nick of time. Miss Sullivan and I kept up a game of guessing which taught me more about the use of language than any set lessons could have done. Every evening, seated round a glowing wood fire, we played our guessing game, which grew more and more exciting as Christmas approached.

On Christmas Eve the Tuscumbia schoolchildren had their tree, to which they invited me. In the centre of the school-room stood a beautiful tree ablaze and shimmering in the soft light, its branches loaded with strange, wonderful fruit. It was a moment of supreme happiness. I danced and capered round the tree in an ecstasy. When I learned that there was a gift for each child, I was delighted, and the kind people who had pre-pared the tree permitted me to hand the presents to the chil-dren. In the pleasure of doing this, I did not stop to look at my own gifts; but when I was ready for them, my impatience for the real Christmas to begin almost got beyond control. I knew the gifts I already had were not those of which friends had thrown out such tantalizing hints, and my teacher said the presents I was to have would be even nicer than these. I was persuaded, however, to content myself with the gifts from the tree and leave the others until morning.

That night, after I had hung my stocking, I lay awake a long time, pretending to be asleep and keeping alert to see what Santa Claus would do when he came. At last I fell asleep with a new doll and a white bear in my arms. Next morning it was I who waked the whole family with my first "Merry Christmas!" I found surprises, not in the stocking only, but on the table, on all the chairs, at the door, on the very window-sill; indeed, I could hardly walk without stumbling on a bit of Christmas wrapped up in tissue paper. But when my teacher presented me with a canary, my cup of happiness overflowed.

Little Tim was so tame that he would hop on my finger and eat candied cherries out of my hand. Miss Sullivan taught me to take all the care of my new pet. Every morning after break-fast I prepared his bath, made his cage clean and sweet, filled his cups with fresh seed and water from the well-house, and hung a spray of chickweed in his swing.

One morning I left the cage on the window-seat while I went to fetch water for his bath. When I returned I felt a big cat brush past me as I opened the door. At first I did not realize what had happened; but when I put my hand in the cage and Tim's pretty wings did not meet my touch or his small pointed claws take hold of my finger, I knew that I should never see my sweet little singer again.

CHAPTER 9

THE NEXT important event in my life was my visit to Boston, in May 1888. As if it were yesterday I remember the preparations, the departure with my teacher and my mother, the journey, and finally the arrival in Boston. How different this journey was from the one I had made to Baltimore two years before! I was no longer a restless, excitable little creature, requiring the attention of everybody on the train to keep me amused. I sat quietly beside Miss Sullivan, taking in with eager interest all that she told me about what she saw out of the car window: the beautiful Tennessee River, the great cottonfields, the hills and woods, and the crowds of laughing negroes at the stations, who waved to the people on the train and brought delicious candy and popcorn balls through the car. On the seat opposite me sat my big rag doll, Nancy, in a new gingham dress and a beruffled sunbonnet, looking at me out of two bead eyes. Sometimes, when I was not absorbed in Miss Sullivan's descriptions, I remembered Nancy's existence and took her up in my arms, but I generally calmed my conscience by making myself believe that she was asleep.

As I shall not have occasion to refer to Nancy again, I wish to tell here a sad experience she had soon after our arrival in Boston. She was covered with dirt—the remains of mud pies I had compelled her to eat, although she had never shown any special liking for them. The laundress at the Perkins Institution secretly carried her off to give her a bath. This was too much for poor Nancy. When I next saw her she was a formless heap of cotton, which I should not have recognized at all except for the two bead eyes which looked out at me reproachfully.

When the train at last pulled into the station at Boston it was as if a beautiful fairy tale had come true. The "once upon a time" was now; the "far-away country" was here.

We had scarcely arrived at the Perkins Institution for the Blind when I began to make friends with the little blind children. It delighted me inexpressibly to find that they knew the manual alphabet. What joy to talk with other children in my own language! Until then I had been like a foreigner speaking through an interpreter. In the school where Laura Bridgman was taught I was in my own country. It took me some time to appreciate the fact that my new friends were blind. I knew I could not see; but it did not seem possible that all the eager, loving children who gathered round me and joined heartily in my frolics were also blind. I remember the surprise and the pain I felt as I noticed that they placed their hands over mine when I talked to them and that they read books with their fingers. Although I had been told this before, and although I understood my own deprivations, yet I had thought vaguely that since they could hear, they must have a sort of "second sight," and I was not prepared to find one child and another and yet another deprived of the same precious gift. But they were so happy and contented that I lost all sense of pain in the pleasure of their companionship.

One day spent with the blind children made me feel thoroughly at home in my new environment, and I looked eagerly from one pleasant experience to another as the days flew swiftly by. I could not quite convince myself that there was much world left, for I regarded Boston as the beginning and the end of creation.

While we were in Boston we visited Bunker Hill, and there I had my first lesson in history. The story of the brave men who had fought on the spot where we stood excited me greatly. I climbed the monument, counting the steps, and wondering as I went higher and yet higher if the soldiers had climbed this great stairway and shot at the enemy on the ground below.

The next day we went to Plymouth by water. This was my first trip on the ocean and my first voyage in a steamboat. How full of life and motion it was! But the rumble of the machinery made me think it was thundering, and I began to cry, because I feared if it rained we should not be able to have our picnic out of doors. I was more interested, I think, in the great rock on which the Pilgrims landed than in anything else in Plymouth. I could touch it, and perhaps that made the coming of the Pilgrims and their toils and great deeds seem more real to me. I have often held in my hand a little model of the Plymouth Rock which a kind gentleman gave me at Pilgrim Hall, and I have fingered its curves, the split in the centre and the embossed figures "1620," and turned over in my mind all that I knew about the wonderful story of the Pilgrims.

How my childish imagination glowed with the splendour of their enterprise! I idealized them as the bravest and most generous men that ever sought a home in a strange land. I thought they desired the freedom of their fellow men as well as their own. I was keenly surprised and disappointed years later to learn of their acts of persecution that make us tingle with shame, even while we glory in the courage and energy that gave us our "Country Beautiful."

Among the many friends I made in Boston were Mr. William Endicott and his daughter. Their kindness to me was the seed from which many pleasant memories have since grown. One day we visited their beautiful home at Beverly Farms. I remember with delight how I went through their rose-garden, how their dogs, big Leo and little curly-haired Fritz with long ears, came to meet me, and how Nimrod, the swiftest of the horses, poked his nose into my hands for a pat and a lump of sugar. I also remember the beach, where for the first time I played in the sand. It was hard, smooth sand, very different from the loose, sharp sand, mingled with kelp and shells, at Brewster. Mr. Endicott told me about the great ships that came sailing by from Boston, bound for Europe. I saw him many times after that, and he was always a good friend to me; indeed, I was thinking of him when I called Boston "the City of Kind Hearts."

CHAPTER 10

JUST BEFORE the Perkins Institution closed for the summer, it was arranged that my teacher and I should spend our vacation at Brewster, on Cape Code, with our dear friend, Mrs. Hopkins. I was delighted, for my mind was full of the prospective joys and of the wonderful stories I had heard about the sea.

My most vivid recollection of that summer is the ocean. I had always lived far inland and had never had so much as a whiff of salt air; but I had read in a big book called "Our World" a description of the ocean which filled me with wonder and an intense longing to touch the mighty sea and feel it roar. So my little heart leaped high with eager excitement when I knew that my wish was at last to be realized.

No sooner had I been helped into my bathing-suit than I sprang out upon the warm sand and without thought of fear plunged into the cool water. I felt the great billows rock and sink. The buoyant motion of the water filled me with an exquisite, quivering joy. Suddenly my ecstasy gave place to terror; for my foot struck against a rock and the next instant there was a rush of water over my head. I thrust out my hands to grasp some support. I clutched at the water and at the seaweed which the waves tossed in my face. But all my frantic efforts were in vain. The waves seemed to be playing a game with me, and tossed me from one to another in their wild frolic. It was fearful! The good, firm earth had slipped from my feet, and everything seemed shut out from this strange, all-enveloping element—life, air, warmth and love. At last, however, the sea, as if weary of its new toy, threw me back on the shore, and in another instant I was clasped in my teacher's arms. Oh, the comfort of the long, tender embrace! As soon as I had recovered from my panic sufficiently to say anything, I demanded: "Who put salt in the water?"

After I had recovered from my first experience in the water, I thought it great fun to sit on a big rock in my bathing-suit and feel wave after wave dash against the rock, sending up a shower of spray which quite covered me. I felt the pebbles rattling as the waves threw their ponderous weight against the shore; the whole beach seemed racked by their terrific onset, and the air throbbed with their pulsations. The breakers would swoop back to gather themselves for a mightier leap, and I clung to the rock, tense, fascinated, as I felt the dash and roar of the rushing sea!

I could never stay long enough on the shore. The tang of the untainted, fresh and free sea air was like a cool, quieting thought, and the shells and pebbles and the seaweed with tiny living creatures attached to it never lost their fascination for me. One day Miss Sullivan attracted my attention to a strange object which she had captured basking in the shallow water. It was a great horseshoe crab—the first one I had ever seen. I felt of him and thought it very strange that he should carry his house on his back. It suddenly occurred to me that he might make a delightful pet; so I seized him by the tail with both hands and carried him home. This feat pleased me highly, as his body was very heavy, and it took all my strength to drag him half a mile. I would not leave Miss Sullivan in peace until she had put the crab in a trough near the well where I was confident he would be secure. But next morning I went to the trough, and lo, he had disappeared! Nobody knew where he had gone, or how he had escaped. My disappointment was bitter at the time; but little by little I came to realize that it was not kind or wise to force this poor dumb creature out of his element, and after awhile I felt happy in the thought that perhaps he had returned to the sea.

CHAPTER 11

IN THE autumn I returned to my Southern home with a heart full of joyous memories. As I recall that visit North I am filled with wonder at the richness and variety of the experiences that cluster about it. It seems to have been the beginning of everything. The treasures of a new, beautiful world were laid at my feet, and I took in pleasure and information at every turn. I lived myself into all things. I was never still a moment; my life was as full of motion as those little insects that crowd a whole existence into one brief day. I met many people who talked with me by spelling into my hand, and thought in joyous sympathy leaped up to meet thought, and behold, a miracle had been wrought! The barren places between my mind and the minds of others blossomed like the rose.

I spent the autumn months with my family at our summer cottage, on a mountain about fourteen miles from Tuscumbia. It was called Fern Quarry, because near it was a limestone quarry, long since abandoned. Three frolicsome little streams ran through it from springs in the rocks above, leaping here and tumbling there in laughing cascades wherever the rocks tried to bar their way. The opening was filled with ferns which completely covered the beds of limestone and in places hid the streams. The rest of the mountain was thickly wooded. Here were great oaks and splendid evergreens with trunks like mossy pillars, from the branches of which hung garlands of ivy and mistletoe, and persimmon trees, the odour of which pervaded every nook and corner of the wood—an illusive, fragrant something that made the heart glad. In places the wild muscadine and scuppernong vines stretched from tree to tree, making arbours which were always full of butterflies and buzzing insects. It was delightful to lose ourselves in the green hollows of that tangled wood in the late afternoon, and to smell the cool, delicious odours that came up from the earth at the close of the day.

Our cottage was a sort of rough camp, beautifully situated on the top of the mountain among oaks and pines. The small rooms were arranged on each side of a long open hall. Round the house was a wide piazza, where the mountain winds blew, sweet with all wood-scents. We lived on the piazza most of the time—there we worked, ate and played. At the back door there was a great butternut tree, round which the steps had been built, and in front the trees stood so close that I could touch them and feel the wind shake their branches, or the leaves twirl downward in the autumn blast.

Many visitors came to Fern Quarry. In the evening, by the campfire, the men played cards and whiled away the hours in talk and sport. They told stories of their wonderful feats with fowl, fish and quadruped—how many wild ducks and turkeys they had shot, what "savage trout" they had caught, and how they had bagged the craftiest foxes, outwitted the most clever 'possums and overtaken the fleetest deer, until I thought that surely the lion, the tiger, the bear and the rest of the wild tribe would not be able to stand before these wily hunters. "Tomorrow to the chase!" was their good-night shout as the circle of merry friends broke up for the night. The men slept in the hall outside our door, and I could feel the deep breathing of the dogs and the hunters as they lay on their improvised beds.

At dawn I was awakened by the smell of coffee, the rattling of guns, and the heavy footsteps of the men as they strode about, promising themselves the greatest luck of the season. I could also feel the stamping of the horses, which they had ridden out from town and hitched under the trees, where they stood all night, neighing loudly, impatient to be off. At last the men mounted, and, as they say in the old songs, away went the steeds with bridles ringing and whips cracking and hounds racing ahead, and away went the champion hunters "with hark and whoop and wild halloo!"

Later in the morning we made preparations for a barbecue. A fire was kindled at the bottom of a deep hole in the ground, big sticks were laid crosswise at the top, and meat was hung from them and turned on spits. Around the fire squatted negroes, driving away the flies with long branches. The savoury odour of the meat made me hungry long before the tables were set.

When the bustle and excitement of preparation was at its height, the hunting party made its appearance, struggling in by twos and threes, the men hot and weary, the horses covered with foam, and the jaded hounds panting and dejected—and not a single kill! Every man declared that he had seen at least one deer, and that the animal had come very close; but however hotly the dogs might pursue the game, however well the guns might be aimed, at the snap of the trigger there was not a deer in sight. They had been as fortunate as the little boy who said he came very near seeing a rabbit—he saw his tracks. The party soon forgot its disappointment, however, and we sat down, not to venison, but to a tamer feast of veal and roast pig.

One summer I had my pony at Fern Quarry. I called him Black Beauty, as I had just read the book, and he resembled his namesake in every way, from his glossy black coat to the white star on his forehead. I spent many of my happiest hours on his back. Occasionally, when it was quite safe, my teacher would let go of the leading-rein, and the pony sauntered on or stopped at his sweet will to eat grass or nibble the leaves of the trees that grew beside the narrow trail.

On mornings when I did not care for the ride, my teacher and I would start after breakfast for a ramble in the woods, and allow ourselves to get lost amid the trees and vines, with no road to follow except the paths made by cows and horses.

Frequently we came upon impassable thickets which forced us to take a roundabout way. We always returned to the cottage with armfuls of laurel, goldenrod, ferns and gorgeous swamp-flowers such as grow only in the South.

Sometimes I would go with Mildred and my little cousins to gather persimmons. I did not eat them; but I loved their fragrance and enjoyed hunting for them in the leaves and grass. We also went nutting, and I helped them open the chestnut burrs and break the shells of hickory-nuts and walnuts—the big, sweet walnuts!

At the foot of the mountain there was a railroad, and the children watched the trains whiz by. Sometimes a terrific whistle brought us to the steps, and Mildred told me in great excitement that a cow or a horse had strayed on the track. About a mile distant there was a trestle spanning a deep gorge. It was very difficult to walk over, the ties were wide apart and so narrow that one felt as if one were walking on knives. I had never crossed it until one day Mildred, Miss Sullivan and I were lost in the woods, and wandered for hours without finding a path.

Suddenly Mildred pointed with her little hand and exclaimed, "There's the trestle!" We would have taken any way rather than this; but it was late and growing dark, and the trestle was a short cut home. I had to feel for the rails with my toe; but I was not afraid, and got on very well, until all at once there came a faint "puff, puff" from the distance.

"I see the train!" cried Mildred, and in another minute it would have been upon us had we not climbed down on the crossbraces while it rushed over our heads. I felt the hot breath from the engine on my face, and the smoke and ashes almost choked us. As the train rumbled by, the trestle shook and swayed until I thought we should be dashed to the chasm below. With the utmost difficulty we regained the track. Long after dark we reached home and found the cottage empty; the family were all out hunting for us.

CHAPTER 12

A FTER MY first visit to Boston, I spent almost every winter in the North. Once I went on a visit to a New England village with its frozen lakes and vast snow fields. It was then that I had opportunities such as had never been mine to enter into the treasures of the snow.

I recall my surprise on discovering that a mysterious hand had stripped the trees and bushes, leaving only here and there a wrinkled leaf. The birds had flown, and their empty nests in the bare trees were filled with snow. Winter was on hill and field. The earth seemed benumbed by his icy touch, and the very spirits of the trees had withdrawn to their roots, and there, curled up in the dark, lay fast asleep. All life seemed to have ebbed away, and even when the sun shone the day was

> *Shrunk and cold,*
> *As if her veins were sapless and old,*
> *And she rose up decrepitly*
> *For a last dim look at earth and sea.*

The withered grass and the bushes were transformed into a forest of icicles.

Then came a day when the chill air portended a snowstorm. We rushed out-of-doors to feel the first few tiny flakes descending. Hour by hour the flakes dropped silently, softly from their airy height to the earth, and the country became more and more level. A snowy night closed upon the world, and in the morning one could scarcely recognize a feature of the landscape. All the roads were hidden, not a single landmark was visible, only a waste of snow with trees rising out of it.

In the evening a wind from the northeast sprang up, and the flakes rushed hither and thither in furious mêlée. Around the great fire we sat and told merry tales, and frolicked, and quite forgot that we were in the midst of a desolate solitude, shut in from all communication with the outside world. But during the night the fury of the wind increased to such a degree that it thrilled us with a vague terror. The rafters creaked and strained, and the branches of the trees surrounding the house rattled and beat against the windows, as the winds rioted up and down the country.

On the third day after the beginning of the storm the snow ceased. The sun broke through the clouds and shone upon a vast, undulating white plain. High mounds, pyramids heaped in fantastic shapes, and impenetrable drifts lay scattered in every direction.

Narrow paths were shoveled through the drifts. I put on my cloak and hood and went out. The air stung my cheeks like fire. Half walking in the paths, half working our way through the lesser drifts, we succeeded in reaching a pine grove just outside a broad pasture. The trees stood motionless and white like figures in a marble frieze. There was no odour of pine-needles. The rays of the sun fell upon the trees, so that the twigs sparkled like diamonds and dropped in showers when we touched them. So dazzling was the light, it penetrated even the darkness that veils my eyes.

As the days wore on, the drifts gradually shrunk, but before they were wholly gone another storm came, so that I scarcely felt the earth under my feet once all winter. At intervals the trees lost their icy covering, and the bulrushes and underbrush were bare; but the lake lay frozen and hard beneath the sun.

Our favourite amusement during that winter was tobogganing. In places the shore of the lake rises abruptly from the water's edge. Down these steep slopes we used to coast. We would get on our toboggan, a boy would give us a shove, and off we went! Plunging through drifts, leaping hollows, swooping down upon the lake, we would shoot across its gleaming surface to the opposite bank. What joy! What exhilarating madness! For one wild, glad moment we snapped the chain that binds us to earth, and joining hands with the winds we felt ourselves divine!

CHAPTER 13

IT WAS in the spring of 1890 that I learned to speak. The impulse to utter audible sounds had always been strong within me. I used to make noises, keeping one hand on my throat while the other hand felt the movements of my lips. I was pleased with anything that made a noise and liked to feel the cat purr and the dog bark. I also liked to keep my hand on a singer's throat, or on a piano when it was being played. Before I lost my sight and hearing, I was fast learning to talk, but after my illness it was found that I had ceased to speak because I could not hear. I used to sit in my mother's lap all day long and keep my hands on her face because it amused me to feel the motions of her lips; and I moved my lips, too, although I had forgotten what talking was. My friends say that I laughed and cried naturally, and for awhile I made many sounds and word-elements, not because they were a means of communication, but because the need of exercising my vocal organs was imperative. There was, however, one word the meaning of which I still remembered, *water*. I pronounced it "wa-wa." Even this became less and less intelligible until the time when Miss Sullivan began to teach me. I stopped using it only after I had learned to spell the word on my fingers.

I had known for a long time that the people about me used a method of communication different from mine; and even before I knew that a deaf child could be taught to speak, I was conscious of dissatisfaction with the means of communication I already possessed. One who is entirely dependent upon the manual alphabet has always a sense of restraint, of narrowness. This feeling began to agitate me with a vexing, forward-reaching sense of a lack that should be filled. My thoughts would often rise and beat up like birds against the wind; and I persisted in using my lips and voice. Friends tried to discourage this tendency, fearing lest it would lead to disappointment. But I persisted, and an accident soon occurred which resulted in the breaking down of this great barrier—I heard the story of Ragnhild Kaata.

In 1890 Mrs. Lamson, who had been one of Laura Bridgman's teachers, and who had just returned from a visit to Norway and Sweden, came to see me, and told me of Ragnhild Kaata, a deaf and blind girl in Norway who had actually been taught to speak. Mrs. Lamson had scarcely finished telling me about this girl's success before I was on fire with eagerness. I resolved that I, too, would learn to speak. I would not rest satisfied until my teacher took me, for advice and assistance, to Miss Sarah Fuller, principal of the Horace Mann School. This lovely, sweet-natured lady offered to teach me herself, and we began the twenty-sixth of March, 1890.

Miss Fuller's method was this: she passed my hand lightly over her face, and let me feel the position of her tongue and lips when she made a sound. I was eager to imitate every motion and in an hour had learned six elements of speech: M, P, A, S, T, I. Miss Fuller gave me eleven lessons in all. I shall never forget the surprise and delight I felt when I uttered my first connected sentence, "It is warm." True, they were broken and stammering syllables; but they were human speech. My soul, conscious of new strength, came out of bondage, and was reaching through those broken symbols of speech to all knowledge and all faith.

No deaf child who has earnestly tried to speak the words which he has never heard—to come out of the prison of silence, where no tone of love, no song of bird, no strain of music ever pierces the stillness—can forget the thrill of surprise, the joy of discovery which came over him when he uttered his first word. Only such a one can appreciate the eagerness with which I talked to my toys, to stones, trees, birds and dumb animals, or the delight I felt when at my call Mildred ran to me or my dogs obeyed my commands. It is an unspeakable boon to me to be able to speak in winged words that need no interpretation. As I talked, happy thoughts fluttered up out of my words that might perhaps have struggled in vain to escape my fingers.

But it must not be supposed that I could really talk in this short time. I had learned only the elements of speech. Miss Fuller and Miss Sullivan could understand me, but most people would not have understood one word in a hundred. Nor is it true that, after I had learned these elements, I did the rest of the work myself. But for Miss Sullivan's genius, untiring perseverance and devotion, I could not have progressed as far as I have toward natural speech. In the first place, I laboured night and day before I could be understood even by my most intimate friends; in the second place, I needed Miss Sullivan's assistance constantly in my efforts to articulate each sound clearly and to combine all sounds in a thousand ways. Even now she calls my attention every day to mispronounced words.

All teachers of the deaf know what this means, and only they can at all appreciate the peculiar difficulties with which I had to contend. I had to use the sense of touch in catching the vibrations of the throat, the movements of the mouth and the expression of the face; and often this sense was at fault. In such cases I was forced to repeat the words or sentences, sometimes for hours, until I felt the proper ring in my own voice. My work was practice, practice, practice. Discouragement and weariness cast me down frequently; but the next moment the thought that I should soon be at home and show my loved ones what I had accomplished spurred me on, and I eagerly looked forward to their pleasure in my achievement.

"My little sister will understand me now," was a thought stronger than all obstacles. I used to repeat ecstatically, "I am not dumb now." I could not be despondent while I anticipated the delight of talking to my mother and reading her responses from her lips. It astonished me to find how much easier it is to talk than to spell with the fingers, and I discarded the manual alphabet as a medium of communication on my part; but Miss Sullivan and a few friends still use it in speaking to me, for it is more convenient and more rapid than lip-reading.

Just here, perhaps, I had better explain our use of the manual alphabet, which seems to puzzle people who do not know us. One who reads or talks to me spells with his hand, using the single-hand manual alphabet generally employed by the deaf. I place my hand on the hand of the speaker so lightly as not to impede its movements. The position of the hand is as easy to feel as it is to see. I do not feel each letter any more than you see each letter separately when you read. Constant practice makes the fingers very flexible, and some of my friends spell rapidly—about as fast as an expert writes on a typewriter. The mere spelling is, of course, no more a conscious act than it is in writing.

When I had made speech my own, I could not wait to go home. At last the happiest of happy moments arrived. I had made my homeward journey, talking constantly to Miss Sullivan, not for the sake of talking, but determined to improve to the last minute. Almost before I knew it, the train stopped at the Tuscumbia station, and there on the platform stood the whole family. My eyes fill with tears now as I think how my mother pressed me close to her, speechless and trembling with delight, taking in every syllable that I spoke, while little Mildred seized my free hand and kissed it and danced, and my father expressed his pride and affection in a big silence. It was as if Isaiah's prophecy had been fulfilled in me. "The mountains and the hills shall break forth before you into singing, and all the trees of the field shall clasp their hands!"

CHAPTER 14

THE WINTER of 1892 was darkened by the one cloud in my childhood's bright sky. Joy deserted my heart, and for a long, long time I lived in doubt, anxiety and fear. Books lost their charm for me, and even now the thought of those dreadful days chills my heart. A little story called "The Frost King," which I wrote and sent to Mr. Anagnos, of the Perkins Institution for the Blind, was at the root of the trouble. In order to make the matter clear, I must set forth the facts connected with this episode, which justice to my teacher and to myself compels me to write.

I wrote the story when I was at home, the autumn after I had learned to speak. We had stayed up at Fern Quarry later than usual. While we were there, Miss Sullivan had described to me the beauties of the late foliage, and it seems that her descriptions revived the memory of a story, which must have been read to me, and which I must have unconsciously retained. I thought then that I was "making up a story," as children say, and I eagerly sat down to write it before the ideas should slip from me. My thoughts flowed easily; I felt a sense of joy in the composition. Words and images came tripping to my finger ends, and as I thought out sentence after sentence, I wrote them on my braille slate. Now, if words and images come to me without effort, it is a pretty sure sign that they are not the offspring of my own mind, but stray waifs that I regretfully dismiss. At that time I eagerly absorbed everything I read without a thought of authorship, and even now I cannot be quite sure of the boundary line between my ideas and those I find in books. I suppose that is because so many of my impressions come to me through the medium of others' eyes and ears.

When the story was finished, I read it to my teacher, and I recall now vividly the pleasure I felt in the more beautiful passages, and my annoyance at being interrupted to have the pronunciation of a word corrected. At dinner it was read to the assembled family, who were surprised that I could write so well. Some one asked me if I had read it in a book.

This question surprised me very much; for I had not the faintest recollection of having had it read to me. I spoke up and said, "Oh, no, it is my story, and I have written it for Mr. Anagnos."

Accordingly I copied the story and sent it to him for his birthday. It was suggested that I should change the title from "Autumn Leaves" to "The Frost King," which I did. I carried the little story to the post-office myself, feeling as if I were walking on air. I little dreamed how cruelly I should pay for that birthday gift.

Mr. Anagnos was delighted with "The Frost King," and published it in one of the Perkins Institution reports. This was the pinnacle of my happiness, from which I was in a little while dashed to earth. I had been in Boston only a short time when it was discovered that a story similar to "The Frost King," called "The Frost Fairies," by Miss Margaret T. Canby, had appeared before I was born in a book called "Birdie and His Friends." The two stories were so much alike in thought and language that it was evident Miss Canby's story had been read to me, and that mine was—a plagiarism. It was difficult to make me understand this; but when I did understand I was astonished and grieved. No child ever drank deeper of the cup of bitterness than I did. I had disgraced myself; I had brought suspicion upon those I loved best. And yet how could it possibly have happened? I racked my brain until I was weary to recall anything about the frost that I had read before I wrote "The Frost King"; but I could remember nothing, except the common reference to Jack Frost, and a poem for children, "The Freaks of the Frost," and I knew I had not used that in my composition.

At first Mr. Anagnos, though deeply troubled, seemed to believe me. He was unusually tender and kind to me, and for a brief space the shadow lifted. To please him I tried not to be unhappy, and to make myself as pretty as possible for the celebration of Washington's birthday, which took place very soon after I received the sad news.

I was to be Ceres in a kind of masque given by the blind girls. How well I remember the graceful draperies that enfolded me, the bright autumn leaves that wreathed my head, and the fruit and grain at my feet and in my hands, and beneath all the gaiety of the masque the oppressive sense of coming ill that made my heart heavy.

The night before the celebration, one of the teachers of the Institution had asked me a question connected with "The Frost King," and I was telling her that Miss Sullivan had talked to me about Jack Frost and his wonderful works. Something I said made her think she detected in my words a confession that I did remember Miss Canby's story of "The Frost Fairies," and she laid her conclusions before Mr. Anagnos, although I had told her most emphatically that she was mistaken.

Mr. Anagnos, who loved me tenderly, thinking that he had been deceived, turned a deaf ear to the pleadings of love and innocence. He believed, or at least suspected, that Miss Sullivan and I had deliberately stolen the bright thoughts of another and imposed them on him to win his admiration. I was brought before a court of investigation composed of the teachers and officers of the Institution, and Miss Sullivan was asked to leave me. Then I was questioned and cross-questioned with what seemed to me a determination on the part of my judges to force me to acknowledge that I remembered having had "The Frost Fairies" read to me. I felt in every question the doubt and suspicion that was in their minds, and I felt, too, that a loved friend was looking at me reproachfully, although I could not have put all this into words. The blood pressed about my thumping heart, and I could scarcely speak, except in monosyllables. Even the consciousness that it was only a dreadful mistake did not lessen my suffering, and when at last I was allowed to leave the room, I was dazed and did not notice my teacher's caresses, or the tender words of my friends, who said I was a brave little girl and they were proud of me.

As I lay in my bed that night, I wept as I hope few children have wept. I felt so cold, I imagined I should die before morning, and the thought comforted me. I think if this sorrow had come to me when I was older, it would have broken my spirit beyond repairing. But the angel of forgetfulness has gathered up and carried away much of the misery and all the bitterness of those sad days.

Miss Sullivan had never heard of "The Frost Fairies" or of the book in which it was published. With the assistance of Dr. Alexander Graham Bell, she investigated the matter carefully, and at last it came out that Mrs. Sophia C. Hopkins had a copy of Miss Canby's "Birdie and His Friends" in 1888, the year that we spent the summer with her at Brewster. Mrs. Hopkins was unable to find her copy; but she has told me that at that time, while Miss Sullivan was away on a vacation, she tried to amuse me by reading from various books, and although she could not remember reading "The Frost Fairies" any more than I, yet she felt sure that "Birdie and His Friends" was one of them. She explained the disappearance of the book by the fact that she had a short time before sold her house and disposed of many juvenile books, such as old schoolbooks and fairy tales, and that "Birdie and His Friends" was probably among them.

The stories had little or no meaning for me then; but the mere spelling of the strange words was sufficient to amuse a little child who could do almost nothing to amuse herself; and although I do not recall a single circumstance connected with the reading of the stories, yet I cannot help thinking that I made a great effort to remember the words, with the intention of having my teacher explain them when she returned. One thing is certain, the language was ineffaceably stamped upon my brain, though for a long time no one knew it, least of all myself.

When Miss Sullivan came back, I did not speak to her about "The Frost Fairies," probably because she began at once to read "Little Lord Fauntleroy," which filled my mind to the exclusion of everything else. But the fact remains that Miss Canby's story was read to me once, and that long after I had forgotten it, it came back to me so naturally that I never suspected that it was the child of another mind.

In my trouble I received many messages of love and sympathy. All the friends I loved best, except one, have remained my own to the present time.

Miss Canby herself wrote kindly, "Some day you will write a great story out of your own head, that will be a comfort and help to many." But this kind prophecy has never been fulfilled. I have never played with words again for the mere pleasure of the game. Indeed, I have ever since been tortured by the fear that what I write is not my own. For a long time, when I wrote a letter, even to my mother, I was seized with a sudden feeling of terror, and I would spell the sentences over and over, to make sure that I had not read them in a book. Had it not been for the persistent encouragement of Miss Sullivan, I think I should have given up trying to write altogether.

I have read "The Frost Fairies" since, also the letters I wrote in which I used other ideas of Miss Canby's. I find in one of them, a letter to Mr. Anagnos, dated September 29, 1891, words and sentiments exactly like those of the book. At the time I was writing "The Frost King," and this letter, like many others, contains phrases which show that my mind was saturated with the story. I represent my teacher as saying to me of the golden autumn leaves, "Yes, they are beautiful enough to comfort us for the flight of summer"—an idea direct from Miss Canby's story.

This habit of assimilating what pleased me and giving it out again as my own appears in much of my early correspondence and my first attempts at writing. In a composition which I wrote about the old cities of Greece and Italy, I borrowed my glowing descriptions, with variations, from sources I have forgotten. I knew Mr. Anagnos's great love of antiquity and his enthusiastic appreciation of all beautiful sentiments about Italy and Greece. I therefore gathered from all the books I read every bit of poetry or of history that I thought would give him pleasure. Mr. Anagnos, in speaking of my composition on the cities, has said, "These ideas are poetic in their essence." But I do not understand how he ever thought a blind and deaf child of eleven could have invented them. Yet I cannot think that because I did not originate the ideas, my little composition is therefore quite devoid of interest. It shows me that I could express my appreciation of beautiful and poetic ideas in clear and animated language.

Those early compositions were mental gymnastics. I was learning, as all young and inexperienced persons learn, by assimilation and imitation, to put ideas into words. Everything I found in books that pleased me I retained in my memory, consciously or unconsciously, and adapted it. The young writer, as Stevenson has said, instinctively tries to copy whatever seems most admirable, and he shifts his admiration with astonishing versatility. It is only after years of this sort of practice that even great men have learned to marshal the legion of words which come thronging through every byway of the mind.

I am afraid I have not yet completed this process. It is certain that I cannot always distinguish my own thoughts from those I read, because what I read becomes the very substance and texture of my mind. Consequently, in nearly all that I write, I produce something which very much resembles the crazy patchwork I used to make when I first learned to sew. This patchwork was made of all sorts of odds and ends— pretty bits of silk and velvet; but the coarse pieces that were not pleasant to touch always predominated. Likewise my compositions are made up of crude notions of my own, inlaid with the brighter thoughts and riper opinions of the authors I have read. It seems to me that the great difficulty of writing is to make the language of the educated mind express our confused ideas, half feelings, half thoughts, when we are little more than bundles of instinctive tendencies. Trying to write is very much like trying to put a Chinese puzzle together. We have a pattern in mind which we wish to work out in words; but the words will not fit the spaces, or, if they do, they will not match the design. But we keep on trying because we know that others have succeeded, and we are not willing to acknowledge defeat.

"There is no way to become original, except to be born so," says Stevenson, and although I may not be original, I hope sometime to outgrow my artificial, periwigged compositions. Then, perhaps, my own thoughts and experiences will come to the surface. Meanwhile I trust and hope and persevere, and try not to let the bitter memory of "The Frost King" trammel my efforts.

So this sad experience may have done me good and set me thinking on some of the problems of composition. My only regret is that it resulted in the loss of one of my dearest friends, Mr. Anagnos.

Since the publication of "The Story of My Life" in the *Ladies' Home Journal*, Mr. Anagnos has made a statement, in a letter to Mr. Macy, that at the time of the "Frost King" matter, he believed I was innocent. He says, the court of investigation before which I was brought consisted of eight people: four blind, four seeing persons. Four of them, he says, thought I knew that Miss Canby's story had been read to me, and the others did not hold this view. Mr. Anagnos states that he cast his vote with those who were favourable to me.

But, however the case may have been, with whichever side he may have cast his vote, when I went into the room where Mr. Anagnos had so often held me on his knee and, forgetting his many cares, had shared in my frolics, and found there persons who seemed to doubt me, I felt that there was something hostile and menacing in the very atmosphere, and subsequent events have borne out this impression. For two years he seems to have held the belief that Miss Sullivan and I were innocent. Then he evidently retracted his favourable judgment, why I do not know. Nor did I know the details of the investigation. I never knew even the names of the members of the "court" who did not speak to me. I was too excited to notice anything, too frightened to ask questions. Indeed, I could scarcely think what I was saying, or what was being said to me.

I have given this account of the "Frost King" affair because it was important in my life and education; and, in order that there might be no misunderstandings, I have set forth all the facts as they appear to me, without a thought of defending myself or of laying blame on any one.

CHAPTER 15

THE SUMMER and winter following the "Frost King" incident I spent with my family in Alabama. I recall with delight that home-going. Everything had budded and blossomed. I was happy. "The Frost King" was forgotten.

When the ground was strewn with the crimson and golden leaves of autumn, and the musk-scented grapes that covered the arbour at the end of the garden were turning golden brown in the sunshine, I began to write a sketch of my life—a year after I had written "The Frost King."

I was still excessively scrupulous about everything I wrote. The thought that what I wrote might not be absolutely my own tormented me. No one knew of these fears except my teacher. A strange sensitiveness prevented me from referring to the "Frost King"; and often when an idea flashed out in the course of conversation I would spell softly to her, "I am not sure it is mine." At other times, in the midst of a paragraph I was writing, I said to myself, "Suppose it should be found that all this was written by some one long ago!" An impish fear clutched my hand, so that I could not write any more that day. And even now I sometimes feel the same uneasiness and disquietude. Miss Sullivan consoled and helped me in every way she could think of; but the terrible experience I had passed through left a lasting impression on my mind, the significance of which I am only just beginning to understand. It was with the hope of restoring my self-confidence that she persuaded me to write for the *Youth's Companion* a brief account of my life. I was then twelve years old. As I look back on my struggle to write that little story, it seems to me that I must have had a prophetic vision of the good that would come of the undertaking, or I should surely have failed.

I wrote timidly, fearfully, but resolutely, urged on by my teacher, who knew that if I persevered, I should find my mental foothold again and get a grip on my faculties. Up to the time of the "Frost King" episode, I had lived the unconscious life of a little child; now my thoughts were turned inward, and I beheld things invisible. Gradually I emerged from the penumbra of that experience with a mind made clearer by trial and with a truer knowledge of life.

The chief events of the year 1893 were my trip to Washington during the inauguration of President Cleveland, and visits to Niagara and the World's Fair. Under such circumstances my studies were constantly interrupted and often put aside for many weeks, so that it is impossible for me to give a connected account of them.

We went to Niagara in March, 1893. It is difficult to describe my emotions when I stood on the point which overhangs the American Falls and felt the air vibrate and the earth tremble.

It seems strange to many people that I should be impressed by the wonders and beauties of Niagara. They are always asking: "What does this beauty or that music mean to you? You cannot see the waves rolling up the beach or hear their roar. What do they mean to you?" In the most evident sense they mean everything. I cannot fathom or define their meaning any more than I can fathom or define love or religion or goodness.

During the summer of 1893, Miss Sullivan and I visited the World's Fair with Dr. Alexander Graham Bell. I recall with unmixed delight those days when a thousand childish fancies became beautiful realities. Every day in imagination I made a trip round the world, and I saw many wonders from the uttermost parts of the earth—marvels of invention, treasuries of industry and skill and all the activities of human life actually passed under my finger tips.

I liked to visit the Midway Plaisance. It seemed like the "Arabian Nights," it was crammed so full of novelty and interest. Here was the India of my books in the curious bazaar with its Shivas and elephant-gods; there was the land of the Pyramids concentrated in a model Cairo with its mosques and its long processions of camels; yonder were the lagoons of Venice, where we sailed every evening when the city and the fountains were illuminated. I also went on board a Viking ship which lay a short distance from the little craft. I had been on a man-of-war before, in Boston, and it interested me to see, on this Viking ship, how the seaman was once all in all—how he sailed and took storm and calm alike with undaunted heart, and gave chase to whosoever reëchoed his cry, "We are of the sea!" and fought with brains and sinews, self-reliant, self-sufficient, instead of being thrust into the background by unintelligent machinery, as Jack is to-day. So it always is—"man only is interesting to man."

At a little distance from this ship there was a model of the *Santa Maria*, which I also examined. The captain showed me Columbus's cabin and the desk with an hour-glass on it. This small instrument impressed me most because it made me think how weary the heroic navigator must have felt as he saw the sand dropping grain by grain while desperate men were plotting against his life.

Mr. Higinbotham, President of the World's Fair, kindly gave me permission to touch the exhibits, and with an eagerness as insatiable as that with which Pizarro seized the treasures of Peru, I took in the glories of the Fair with my fingers. It was a sort of tangible kaleidoscope, this white city of the

West. Everything fascinated me, especially the French bronzes. They were so lifelike, I thought they were angel visions which the artist had caught and bound in earthly forms.

At the Cape of Good Hope exhibit, I learned much about the processes of mining diamonds. Whenever it was possible, I touched the machinery while it was in motion, so as to get a clearer idea how the stones were weighed, cut, and polished. I searched in the washings for a diamond and found it myself—the only true diamond, they said, that was ever found in the United States.

Dr. Bell went everywhere with us and in his own delightful way described to me the objects of greatest interest. In the electrical building we examined the telephones, autophones, phonographs, and other inventions, and he made me understand how it is possible to send a message on wires that mock space and outrun time, and, like Prometheus, to draw fire from the sky. We also visited the anthropological department, and I was much interested in the relics of ancient Mexico, in the rude stone implements that are so often the only record of an age—the simple monuments of nature's unlettered children (so I thought as I fingered them) that seem bound to last while the memorials of kings and sages crumble in dust away—and in the Egyptian mummies, which I shrank from touching. From these relics I learned more about the progress of man than I have heard or read since.

All these experiences added a great many new terms to my vocabulary, and in the three weeks I spent at the Fair I took a long leap from the little child's interest in fairy tales and toys to the appreciation of the real and the earnest in the workaday world.

CHAPTER 16

BEFORE OCTOBER, 1893, I had studied various subjects by myself in a more or less desultory manner. I read the histories of Greece, Rome and the United States. I had a French grammar in raised print, and as I already knew some French, I often amused myself by composing in my head short exercises, using the new words as I came across them, and ignoring rules and other technicalities as much as possible. I even tried, without aid, to master the French pronunciation, as I found all the letters and sounds described in the book. Of course this was tasking slender powers for great ends; but it gave me something to do on a rainy day, and I acquired a sufficient knowledge of French to read with pleasure La Fontaine's "Fables," "Le Médecin Malgré Lui" and passages from "Athalie."

I also gave considerable time to the improvement of my speech. I read aloud to Miss Sullivan and recited passages from my favourite poets, which I had committed to memory; she corrected my pronunciation and helped me to phrase and inflect. It was not, however, until October, 1893, after I had recovered from the fatigue and excitement of my visit to the World's Fair, that I began to have lessons in special subjects at fixed hours.

Miss Sullivan and I were at that time in Hulton, Pennsylvania, visiting the family of Mr. William Wade. Mr. Irons, a neighbour of theirs, was a good Latin scholar; it was arranged that I should study under him. I remember him as a man of rare, sweet nature and of wide experience. He taught me Latin grammar principally; but he often helped me in arithmetic, which I found as troublesome as it was uninteresting. Mr. Irons also read with me Tennyson's "In Memoriam." I had read many books before, but never from a critical point of view. I learned for the first time to know an author, to recognize his style as I recognize the clasp of a friend's hand.

At first I was rather unwilling to study Latin grammar. It seemed absurd to waste time analyzing every word I came across—noun, genitive, singular, feminine—when its meaning was quite plain. I thought I might just as well describe my pet in order to know it—order, vertebrate; division, quadruped; class, mammalia; genus, felinus; species, cat, individual, Tabby. But as I got deeper into the subject, I became more interested, and the beauty of the language delighted me. I often amused myself by reading Latin passages, picking up words I understood and trying to make sense. I have never ceased to enjoy this pastime.

There is nothing more beautiful, I think, than the evanescent fleeting images and sentiments presented by a language one is just becoming familiar with—ideas that flit across the mental sky, shaped and tinted by capricious fancy. Miss Sullivan sat beside me at my lessons, spelling into my hand whatever Mr. Irons said, and looking up new words for me. I was just beginning to read Caesar's "Gallic War" when I went to my home in Alabama.

CHAPTER 17

IN THE summer of 1894, I attended the meeting at Chautauqua of the American Association to Promote the Teaching of Speech to the Deaf. There it was arranged that I should go to the Wright-Humason School for the Deaf in New York City. I went there in October, 1894, accompanied by Miss Sullivan. This school was chosen especially for the purpose of obtaining the highest advantages in vocal culture and training in lip-reading. In addition to my work in these subjects, I studied, during the two years I was in the school, arithmetic, physical geography, French and German.

Miss Reamy, my German teacher, could use the manual alphabet, and after I had acquired a small vocabulary, we talked together in German whenever we had a chance, and in a few months I could understand almost everything she said. Before the end of the first year I read "Wilhelm Tell" with the greatest delight. Indeed, I think I made more progress in German than in any of my mother studies. I found French much more difficult. I studied it with Madame Olivier, a French lady who did not know the manual alphabet, and who was obliged to give her instruction orally. I could not read her lips easily; so my progress was much slower than in German. I managed, however, to read "Le Médecin Malgré Lui" again. It was very amusing but I did not like it nearly so well as "Wilhelm Tell."

My progress in lip-reading and speech was not what my teachers and I had hoped and expected it would be. It was my ambition to speak like other people, and my teachers believed that this could be accomplished; but, although we worked hard and faithfully, yet we did not quite reach our goal. I suppose we aimed too high, and disappointment was therefore inevitable. I still regarded arithmetic as a system of pitfalls. I hung about the dangerous frontier of "guess," avoiding with infinite trouble to myself and others the broad valley of reason. When I was not guessing, I was jumping at conclusions, and this fault, in addition to my dullness, aggravated my difficulties more than was right or necessary.

But although these disappointments caused me great depression at times, I pursued my other studies with unflagging interest, especially physical geography. It was a joy to learn the secrets of nature: how—in the picturesque language of the Old Testament—the winds are made to blow from the four corners of the heavens, how the vapours ascend from the ends of the earth, how rivers are cut out among the rocks, and mountains overturned by the roots, and in what ways man may overcome many forces mightier than himself. The two years in New York were happy ones, and I look back to them with genuine pleasure.

I remember especially the walks we all took together every day in Central Park, the only part of the city that was congenial to me. I never lost a jot of my delight in this great park. I loved to have it described every time I entered it; for it was beautiful in all its aspects, and these aspects were so many that it was beautiful in a different way each day of the nine months I spent in New York.

In the spring we made excursions to various places of interest. We sailed on the Hudson River and wandered about on its green banks, of which Bryant loved to sing. I liked the simple wild grandeur of the palisades. Among the places I visited were West Point, Tarrytown, the home of Washington Irving, where I walked through "Sleepy Hollow."

The teachers at the Wright-Humason School were always planning how they might give the pupils every advantage that those who hear enjoy—how they might make much of few tendencies and passive memories in the cases of the little ones—and lead them out of the cramping circumstances in which their lives were set.

Before I left New York, these bright days were darkened by the greatest sorrow that I have ever borne, except the death of my father. Mr. John P. Spaulding, of Boston, died in February, 1896. Only those who knew and loved him best can understand what his friendship meant to me. He, who made every one happy in a beautiful, unobtrusive way, was most kind and tender to Miss Sullivan and me. So long as we felt his loving presence and knew that he took a watchful interest in our work, fraught with so many difficulties, we could not be discouraged. His going away left a vacancy in our lives that has never been filled.

CHAPTER 18

I N OCTOBER, 1896, I entered the Cambridge School for Young Ladies, to be prepared for Radcliffe.

When I was a little girl, I visited Wellesley and surprised my friends by the announcement, "Some day I shall go to college—but I shall go to Harvard!" When asked why I would not go to Wellesley, I replied that there were only girls there. The thought of going to college took root in my heart and became an earnest desire, which impelled me to enter into competition for a degree with seeing and hearing girls, in the face of the strong opposition of many true and wise friends. When I left New York the idea had become a fixed purpose; and it was decided that I should go to Cambridge. This was the nearest approach I could get to Harvard and to the fulfillment of my childish declaration.

At the Cambridge School the plan was to have Miss Sullivan attend the classes with me and interpret to me the instruction given.

Of course my instructors had had no experience in teaching any but normal pupils, and my own means of conversing with them was reading their lips. My studies for the first year were English history, English literature, German, Latin, arithmetic, Latin composition and occasional themes. Until then I had never taken a course of study with the idea of preparing for college; but I had been well drilled in English by Miss Sullivan, and it soon became evident to my teachers that I needed no special instruction in this subject beyond a critical study of the books prescribed by the college. I had had, moreover, a good start in French, and received six months' instruction in Latin; but German was the subject with which I was most familiar.

In spite, however, of these advantages, there were serious drawbacks to my progress. Miss Sullivan could not spell out in my hand all that the books required, and it was very difficult to have the text-books embossed in time to be of use to me, although my friends in London and Philadelphia were willing to hasten the work. For a while, indeed, I had to copy my Latin in braille, so that I could recite with the other girls. My instructors soon became sufficiently familiar with my imperfect speech to answer my questions readily and correct mistakes. I could not make notes in class or write exercises; but I wrote all my compositions and translations at home on my typewriter.

Each day Miss Sullivan went to the classes with me and spelled into my hand with infinite patience all that the teachers said. In study hours she had to look up new words for me and read and reread notes and books I did not have in raised print. The tedium of that work is hard to conceive. Frau Gröte, my German teacher, and Mr. Gilman, the principal, were the only teachers in the school who learned the finger alphabet to give me instruction. No one realized more fully than dear Frau Gröte how slow and inadequate her spelling was. Nevertheless, in the goodness of her heart she laboriously spelled out her instructions to me in special lessons twice a week, to give Miss Sullivan a little rest. But, though everybody was kind and ready to help us, there was only one hand that could turn drudgery into pleasure.

That year I finished arithmetic, reviewed my Latin grammar, and read three chapters of Caesar's "Gallic War." In German I read, partly with my fingers and partly with Miss Sullivan's assistance, Schiller's "Lied von der Glocke" and "Taucher," Heine's "Harzreise," Freytag's "Aus dem Staat Friedrichs des Grossen," Riehl's "Fluch Der Schönheit," Lessing's "Minna von Barnhelm," and Goethe's "Aus meinem Leben." I took the greatest delight in these German books, especially Schiller's wonderful lyrics, the history of

Frederick the Great's magnificent achievements and the account of Goethe's life. I was sorry to finish "Die Harzreise," so full of happy witticisms and charming descriptions of vine-clad hills, streams that sing and ripple in the sunshine, and wild regions, sacred to tradition and legend, the gray sisters of a long-vanished, imaginative age—descriptions such as can be given only by those to whom nature is "a feeling, a love and an appetite."

Mr. Gilman instructed me part of the year in English literature. We read together, "As You Like It," Burke's "Speech on Conciliation with America," and Macaulay's "Life of Samuel Johnson." Mr. Gilman's broad views of history and literature and his clever explanations made my work easier and pleasanter than it could have been had I only read notes mechanically with the necessarily brief explanations given in the classes.

Burke's speech was more instructive than any other book on a political subject that I had ever read. My mind stirred with the stirring times, and the characters round which the life of two contending nations centred seemed to move right before me. I wondered more and more, while Burke's masterly speech rolled on in mighty surges of eloquence, how it was that King George and his ministers could have turned a deaf ear to his warning prophecy of our victory and their humiliation. Then I entered into the melancholy details of the relation in which the great statesman stood to his party and to the representatives of the people. I thought how strange it was that such precious seeds of truth and wisdom should have fallen among the tares of ignorance and corruption.

In a different way Macaulay's "Life of Samuel Johnson" was interesting. My heart went out to the lonely man who ate the bread of affliction in Grub Street, and yet, in the midst of toil and cruel suffering of body and soul, always had a kind word, and lent a helping hand to the poor and despised. I rejoiced over all his successes, I shut my eyes to his faults, and wondered, not that he had them, but that they had not crushed or dwarfed his soul. But in spite of Macaulay's brilliancy and his admirable faculty of making the commonplace seem fresh and picturesque, his positiveness wearied me at times, and his frequent sacrifices of truth to effect kept me in a questioning attitude very unlike the attitude of reverence in which I had listened to the Demosthenes of Great Britain.

At the Cambridge School, for the first time in my life, I enjoyed the companionship of seeing and hearing girls of my own age. I lived with several others in one of the pleasant houses connected with the school, the house where Mr. Howells used to live, and we all had the advantage of home life. I joined them in many of their games, even blind man's buff and frolics in the snow; I took long walks with them; we discussed our studies and read aloud the things that interested us. Some of the girls learned to speak to me, so that Miss Sullivan did not have to repeat their conversation.

At Christmas, my mother and little sister spent the holidays with me, and Mr. Gilman kindly offered to let Mildred study in his school. So Mildred stayed with me in Cambridge, and for six happy months we were hardly ever apart. It makes me most happy to remember the hours we spent helping each other in study and sharing our recreation together.

I took my preliminary examinations for Radcliffe from the 29th of June to the 3rd of July in 1897. The subjects I offered were Elementary and Advanced German, French, Latin, English, and Greek and Roman history, making nine hours in all. I passed in everything, and received "honours" in German and English.

Perhaps an explanation of the method that was in use when I took my examinations will not be amiss here. The student was required to pass in sixteen hours—twelve hours being called elementary and four advanced. He had to pass five hours at a time to have them counted. The examination papers were given out at nine o'clock at Harvard and brought to Radcliffe by a special messenger. Each candidate was known, not by his name, but by a number. I was No. 233, but, as I had to use a typewriter, my identity could not be concealed.

It was thought advisable for me to have my examinations

in a room by myself, because the noise of the typewriter might disturb the other girls. Mr. Gilman read all the papers to me by means of the manual alphabet. A man was placed on guard at the door to prevent interruption.

The first day I had German, Mr. Gilman sat beside me and read the paper through first, then sentence by sentence, while I repeated the words aloud, to make sure that I understood him perfectly. The papers were difficult, and I felt very anxious as I wrote out my answers on the typewriter. Mr. Gilman spelled to me what I had written, and I made such changes as I thought necessary, and he inserted them. I wish to say here that I have not had this advantage since in any of my examinations. At Radcliffe no one reads the papers to me after they are written, and I have no opportunity to correct errors unless I finish before the time is up. In that case I correct only such mistakes as I can recall in the few minutes allowed, and make notes of these corrections at the end of my paper. If I passed with higher credit in the preliminaries than in the finals, there are two reasons. In the finals, no one read my work over to me, and in the preliminaries I offered subjects with some of which I was in a measure familiar before my work in the Cambridge school; for at the beginning of the year I had passed examinations in English, History, French and German, which Mr. Gilman gave me from previous Harvard papers.

Mr. Gilman sent my written work to the examiners with a certificate that I, candidate No. 233, had written the papers.

All the other preliminary examinations were conducted in the same manner. None of them was so difficult as the first. I remember that the day the Latin paper was brought to us, Professor Schilling came in and informed me I had passed satisfactorily in German. This encouraged me greatly, and I sped on to the end of the ordeal with a light heart and a steady hand.

CHAPTER 19

WHEN I began my second year at the Gilman school, I was full of hope and determination to succeed. But during the first few weeks I was confronted with unforeseen difficulties. Mr. Gilman had agreed that that year I should study mathematics principally. I had physics, algebra, geometry, astronomy, Greek and Latin. Unfortunately, many of the books I needed had not been embossed in time for me to begin with the classes, and I lacked important apparatus for some of my studies. The classes I was in were very large and it was impossible for the teachers to give me special instruction. Miss Sullivan was obliged to read all the books to me, and interpret for the instructors, and for the first time in eleven years it seemed as if her dear hand would not be equal to the task.

It was necessary for me to write algebra and geometry in class and solve problems in physics, and this I could not do until we bought a braille writer, by means of which I could put down the steps and processes of my work. I could not follow with my eyes the geometrical figures drawn on the blackboard, and my only means of getting a clear idea of them was to make them on a cushion with straight and curved wires, which had bent and pointed ends. I had to carry in my mind, as Mr. Keith says in his report, the lettering of the figures, the hypothesis and conclusion, the construction and the process of the proof. In a word, every study had its obstacles. Sometimes I lost all courage and betrayed my feelings in a way I am ashamed to remember, especially as the signs of my trouble were afterward used against Miss Sullivan, the only person of all the kind friends I had there, who could make the crooked straight and the rough places smooth.

Little by little, however, my difficulties began to disappear. The embossed books and other apparatus arrived, and I threw myself into the work with renewed confidence. Algebra and geometry were the only studies that continued to defy my efforts to comprehend them. As I have said before, I had no aptitude for mathematics; the different points were not explained to me as fully as I wished. The geometrical diagrams were particularly vexing because I could not see the relation of the different parts to one another, even on the cushion. It was not until Mr. Keith taught me that I had a clear idea of mathematics.

I was beginning to overcome these difficulties when an event occurred which changed everything.

Just before the books came, Mr. Gilman had begun to remonstrate with Miss Sullivan on the ground that I was working too hard, and in spite of my earnest protestations, he reduced the number of my recitations. At the beginning we had agreed that I should, if necessary, take five years to prepare for college, but at the end of the first year the success of my examinations showed Miss Sullivan, Miss Harbaugh (Mr. Gilman's head teacher), and one other, that I could without too much effort complete my preparation in two years more. Mr. Gilman at first agreed to this; but when my tasks had become somewhat perplexing, he insisted that I was overworked, and that I should remain at his school three years longer. I did not like his plan, for I wished to enter college with my class.

On the seventeenth of November I was not very well, and did not go to school. Although Miss Sullivan knew that my indisposition was not serious, yet Mr. Gilman, on hearing of it, declared that I was breaking down and made changes in my studies which would have rendered it impossible for me to take my final examinations with my class. In the end the difference of opinion between Mr. Gilman and Miss Sullivan resulted in my mother's withdrawing my sister Mildred and me from the Cambridge School.

After some delay it was arranged that I should continue my studies under a tutor, Mr. Merton S. Keith, of Cambridge. Miss Sullivan and I spent the rest of the winter with our friends, the Chamberlins in Wrentham, twenty-five miles from Boston.

From February to July, 1898, Mr. Keith came out to Wrentham twice a week, and taught me algebra, geometry, Greek and Latin. Miss Sullivan interpreted his instruction.

In October, 1898, we returned to Boston. For eight months Mr. Keith gave me lessons five times a week, in periods of about an hour. He explained each time what I did not understand in the previous lesson, assigned new work, and took home with him the Greek exercises which I had written during the week on my typewriter, corrected them fully, and returned them to me.

In this way my preparation for college went on without interruption. I found it much easier and pleasanter to be taught by myself than to receive instruction in class. There was no hurry, no confusion. My tutor had plenty of time to explain what I did not understand, so I got on faster and did better work than I ever did in school. I still found more difficulty in mastering problems in mathematics than I did in any other of my studies. I wish algebra and geometry had been half as easy as the languages and literature. But even mathematics Mr. Keith made interesting; he succeeded in whittling problems small enough to get through my brain. He kept my mind alert and eager, and trained it to reason clearly, and to seek conclusions calmly and logically, instead of jumping wildly into space and arriving nowhere. He was always gentle and forbearing, no matter how dull I might be, and believe me, my stupidity would often have exhausted the patience of Job.

On the 29th and 30th of June, 1899, I took my final examinations for Radcliffe College. The first day I had Elementary Greek and Advanced Latin, and the second day Geometry, Algebra and Advanced Greek.

The college authorities did not allow Miss Sullivan to read the examination papers to me; so Mr. Eugene C. Vining, one of the instructors at the Perkins Institution for the Blind, was employed to copy the papers for me in American braille. Mr. Vining was a stranger to me, and could not communicate with me, except by writing braille. The proctor was also a stranger, and did not attempt to communicate with me in any way.

The braille worked well enough in the languages, but when it came to geometry and algebra, difficulties rose. I was sorely perplexed, and felt discouraged wasting much precious time, especially in algebra. It is true that I was familiar with all literary braille in common use in this country—English, American, and New York Point; but the various signs and symbols in geometry and algebra in the three systems are very different, and I had used only the English braille in my algebra.

Two days before the examinations, Mr. Vining sent me a braille copy of one of the old Harvard papers in algebra. To my dismay I found that it was in the American notation. I sat down immediately and wrote to Mr. Vining, asking him to explain the signs. I received another paper and a table of signs by return mail, and I set to work to learn the notation. But on the night before the algebra examination, while I was struggling over some very complicated examples, I could not tell the combinations of bracket, brace and radical. Both Mr. Keith and I were distressed and full of forebodings for the morrow; but we went over to the college a little before the examination began, and had Mr. Vining explain more fully the American symbols.

In geometry my chief difficulty was that I had always been accustomed to read the propositions in line print, or to have them spelled into my hand; and somehow, although the propositions were right before me, I found the braille confusing, and could not fix clearly in my mind what I was reading. But when I took up algebra I had a harder time still. The signs, which I had so lately learned, and which I thought I knew, perplexed me. Besides, I could not see what I wrote on my typewriter. I had always done my work in braille or in my head. Mr. Keith had relied too much on my ability to solve problems mentally, and had not trained me to write examination papers. Consequently my work was painfully slow, and I had to read the examples over and over before I could form any idea of what I was required to do. Indeed, I am not sure now that I read all the signs correctly. I found it very hard to keep my wits about me.

But I do not blame any one. The administrative board of Radcliffe did not realize how difficult they were making my examinations, nor did they understand the peculiar difficulties I had to surmount. But if they unintentionally placed obstacles in my way, I have the consolation of knowing that I overcame them all.

CHAPTER 20

THE STRUGGLE for admission to college was ended, and I could now enter Radcliffe whenever I pleased. Before I entered college, however, it was thought best that I should study another year under Mr. Keith. It was not, therefore, until the fall of 1900 that my dream of going to college was realized.

I remember my first day at Radcliffe. It was a day full of interest for me. I had looked forward to it for years. A potent force within me, stronger than the persuasion of my friends, stronger even than the pleadings of my heart, had impelled me to try my strength by the standards of those who see and hear. I knew that there were obstacles in the way; but I was eager to overcome them. I had taken to heart the words of the wise Roman who said, "To be banished from Rome is but to

live outside of Rome." Debarred from the great highways of
knowledge, I was compelled to make the journey across
country by unfrequented roads—that was all; and I knew that
in college there were many bypaths where I could touch
hands with girls who were thinking, loving and struggling
like me.

I began my studies with eagerness. Before me I saw a new
world opening in beauty and light, and I felt within me the capacity to know all things. In the wonderland of Mind I should
be as free as another. Its people, scenery, manners, joys,
tragedies should be living, tangible interpreters of the real
world. The lecture-halls seemed filled with the spirit of the
great and the wise, and I thought the professors were the em-
bodiment of wisdom. If I have since learned differently, I am
not going to tell anybody.

But I soon discovered that college was not quite the romantic lyceum I had imagined. Many of the dreams that had
delighted my young inexperience became beautifully less and
"faded into the light of common day." Gradually I began to
find that there were disadvantages in going to college.

The one I felt and still feel most is lack of time. I used to
have time to think, to reflect, my mind and I. We would sit
together of an evening and listen to the inner melodies of
the spirit, which one hears only in leisure moments when the
words of some loved poet touch a deep, sweet chord in the
soul that until then had been silent. But in college there is no
time to commune with one's thoughts. One goes to college to
learn, it seems, not to think. When one enters the portals of
learning, one leaves the dearest pleasures—solitude, books
and imagination—outside with the whistling pines. I suppose
I ought to find some comfort in the thought that I am laying
up treasures for future enjoyment, but I am improvident
enough to prefer present joy to hoarding riches against a
rainy day.

My studies the first year were French, German, history,
English composition and English literature. In the French
course I read some of the works of Corneille, Molière,
Racine, Alfred de Musset and Sainte-Beuve, and in the

German those of Goethe and Schiller. I reviewed rapidly the whole period of history from the fall of the Roman Empire to the eighteenth century, and in English literature studied critically Milton's poems and "Areopagitica."

I am frequently asked how I overcome the peculiar conditions under which I work in college. In the classroom I am of course practically alone. The professor is as remote as if he were speaking through a telephone. The lectures are spelled into my hand as rapidly as possible, and much of the individuality of the lecturer is lost to me in the effort to keep in the race. The words rush through my hands like hounds in pursuit of a hare which they often miss. But in this respect I do not think I am much worse off than the girls who take notes. If the mind is occupied with the mechanical process of hearing and putting words on paper at pell-mell speed, I should not think one could pay much attention to the subject under consideration or the manner in which it is presented. I cannot make notes during the lectures, because my hands are busy listening. Usually I jot down what I can remember of them when I get home. I write the exercises, daily themes, criticisms and hour-tests, the mid-year and final examinations, on my typewriter, so that the professors have no difficulty in finding out how little I know. When I began the study of Latin prosody, I devised and explained to my professor a system of signs indicating the different meters and quantities.

I use the Hammond typewriter. I have tried many machines, and I find the Hammond is the best adapted to the peculiar needs of my work. With this machine movable type shuttles can be used, and one can have several shuttles, each with a different set of characters—Greek, French, or mathematical, according to the kind of writing one wishes to do on the typewriter. Without it, I doubt if I could go to college.

Very few of the books required in the various courses are printed for the blind, and I am obliged to have them spelled into my hand. Consequently I need more time to prepare my lessons than other girls. The manual part takes longer, and I have perplexities which they have not. There are days when the close attention I must give to details chafes my spirit, and the thought that I must spend hours reading a few chapters, while in the world without other girls are laughing and singing and dancing, makes me rebellious; but I soon recover my buoyancy and laugh the discontent out of my heart. For, after all, every one who wishes to gain true knowledge must climb the Hill Difficulty alone, and since there is no royal road to the summit, I must zigzag it in my own way. I slip back many times, I fall, I stand still, I run against the edge of hidden obstacles, I lose my temper and find it again and keep it better. I trudge on, I gain a little, I feel encouraged, I get more eager and climb higher and begin to see the widening horizon. Every struggle is a victory. One more effort and I reach the luminous cloud, the blue depths of the sky, the uplands of my desire. I am not always alone, however, in these struggles. Mr. William Wade and Mr. E. E. Allen, Principal of the Pennsylvania Institution for the Instruction of the Blind, get for me many of the books I need in raised print. Their thoughtfulness has been more of a help and encouragement to me than they can ever know.

Last year, my second year at Radcliffe, I studied English composition, the Bible as English literature, the governments of America and Europe, the Odes of Horace, and Latin comedy. The class in composition was the pleasantest. It was very lively. The lectures were always interesting, vivacious, witty; for the instructor, Mr. Charles Townsend Copeland, more than any one else I have had until this year, brings before you literature in all its original freshness and power. For one short hour you are permitted to drink in the eternal beauty of the old masters without needless interpretation or exposition. You revel in their fine thoughts. You enjoy with all your soul the sweet thunder of the Old Testament, forgetting the existence of Jahweh and Elohim; and you go home feeling that you have had "a glimpse of that perfection in which spirit and form dwell in immortal harmony; truth and beauty bearing a new growth on the ancient stem of time."

This year is the happiest because I am studying subjects

that especially interest me, economics, Elizabethan literature, Shakespeare under Professor George L. Kittredge, and the History of Philosophy under Professor Josiah Royce. Through philosophy one enters with sympathy of comprehension into the traditions of remote ages and other modes of thought, which erewhile seemed alien and without reason.

But college is not the universal Athens I thought it was. There one does not meet the great and the wise face to face; one does not even feel their living touch. They are there, it is true; but they seem mummified. We must extract them from the crannied wall of learning and dissect and analyze them before we can be sure that we have a Milton or an Isaiah, and not merely a clever imitation. Many scholars forget, it seems to me, that our enjoyment of the great works of literature depends more upon the depth of our sympathy than upon our understanding. The trouble is that very few of their laborious explanations stick in the memory. The mind drops them as a branch drops its overripe fruit. It is possible to know a flower, root and stem and all, and all the processes of growth, and yet to have no appreciation of the flower fresh bathed in heaven's dew. Again and again I ask impatiently, "Why concern myself with these explanations and hypotheses?" They fly hither and thither in my thought like blind birds beating the air with ineffectual wings. I do not mean to object to a thorough knowledge of the famous works we read. I object only to the interminable comments and bewildering criticisms that teach but one thing: there are as many opinions as there are men. But when a great scholar like Professor Kittredge interprets what the master said, it is "as if new sight were given the blind." He brings back Shakespeare, the poet.

There are, however, times when I long to sweep away half the things I am expected to learn; for the overtaxed mind cannot enjoy the treasure it has secured at the greatest cost. It is impossible, I think, to read in one day four or five different books in different languages and treating of widely different subjects, and not lose sight of the very ends for which one reads. When one reads hurriedly and nervously, having in

mind written tests and examinations, one's brain becomes en-
cumbered with a lot of choice bric-a-brac for which there
seems to be little use. At the present time my mind is so full
of heterogeneous matter that I almost despair of ever being
able to put it in order. Whenever I enter the region that was
the kingdom of my mind I feel like the proverbial bull in the
china shop. A thousand odds and ends of knowledge come
crashing about my head like hailstones, and when I try to escape them, theme-goblins and college nixies of all sorts pursue me, until I wish—oh, may I be forgiven the wicked
wish!—that I might smash the idols I came to worship.

But the examinations are the chief bugbears of my college
life. Although I have faced them many times and cast them
down and made them bite the dust, yet they rise again and
menace me with pale looks, until like Bob Acres I feel my
courage oozing out at my finger ends. The days before these
ordeals take place are spent in cramming your mind with
mystic formulae and indigestible dates—unpalatable diets,
until you wish that books and science and you were buried in
the depths of the sea.

At last the dreaded hour arrives, and you are a favoured
being indeed if you feel prepared, and are able at the right
time to call to your standard thoughts that will aid you in that
supreme effort. It happens too often that your trumpet call is
unheeded. It is most perplexing and exasperating that just at
the moment when you need your memory and a nice sense of
discrimination, these faculties take to themselves wings and
fly away. The facts you have garnered with such infinite trouble invariably fail you at a pinch.

"Give a brief account of Huss and his work." Huss? Who
was he and what did he do? The name looks strangely familiar.
You ransack your budget of historic facts much as you would
hunt for a bit of silk in a rag-bag. You are sure it is somewhere
in your mind near the top—you saw it there the other day
when you were looking up the beginnings of the Reformation.
But where is it now? You fish out all manner of odds and
ends of knowledge—revolutions, schisms, massacres, systems

of government; but Huss—where is he? You are amazed at all the things you know which are not on the examination paper. In desperation you seize the budget and dump everything out, and there in a corner is your man, serenely brooding on his own private thought, unconscious of the catastrophe which he has brought upon you.

Just then the proctor informs you that the time is up. With a feeling of intense disgust you kick the mass of rubbish into a corner and go home, your head full of revolutionary schemes to abolish the divine right of professors to ask questions without the consent of the questioned.

It comes over me that in the last two or three pages of this chapter I have used figures which will turn the laugh against me. Ah, here they are—the mixed metaphors mocking and strutting about before me, pointing to the bull in the china shop assailed by hailstones and the bugbears with pale looks, an unanalyzed species! Let them mock on. The words describe so exactly the atmosphere of jostling, tumbling ideas I live in that I will wink at them for once, and put on a deliberate air to say that my ideas of college have changed.

While my days at Radcliffe were still in the future, they were encircled with a halo of romance, which they have lost; but in the transition from romantic to actual I have learned many things I should never have known had I not tried the experiment. One of them is the precious science of patience, which teaches us that we should take our education as we would take a walk in the country, leisurely, our minds hospitably open to impressions of every sort. Such knowledge floods the soul unseen with a soundless tidal wave of deepening thought. "Knowledge is power." Rather, knowledge is happiness, because to have knowledge—broad, deep knowledge—is to know true ends from false, and lofty things from low. To know the thoughts and deeds that have marked man's progress is to feel the great heart-throbs of humanity through the centuries; and if one does not feel in these pulsations a heavenward striving, one must indeed be deaf to the harmonies of life.

CHAPTER 21

I HAVE THUS far sketched the events of my life, but I have not shown how much I have depended on books not only for pleasure and for the wisdom they bring to all who read, but also for that knowledge which comes to others through their eyes and their ears. Indeed, books have meant so much more in my education than in that of others, that I shall go back to the time when I began to read.

I read my first connected story in May 1887, when I was seven years old, and from that day to this I have devoured everything in the shape of a printed page that has come within the reach of my hungry finger tips. As I have said, I did not study regularly during the early years of my education; nor did I read according to rule.

At first I had only a few books in raised print—"readers" for beginners, a collection of stories for children, and a book about the earth called "Our World." I think that was all; but I read them over and over, until the words were so worn and pressed I could scarcely make them out. Sometimes Miss Sullivan read to me, spelling into my hand little stories and poems that she knew I should understand; but I preferred reading myself to being read to, because I liked to read again and again the things that pleased me.

It was during my first visit to Boston that I really began to read in good earnest. I was permitted to spend a part of each day in the Institution library, and to wander from bookcase to bookcase, and take down whatever book my fingers lighted upon. And read I did, whether I understood one word in ten or two words on a page. The words themselves fascinated me; but I took no conscious account of what I read. My mind must, however, have been very impressionable at that period, for it retained many words and whole sentences, to the meaning of which I had not the faintest clue; and afterward, when I began to talk and write, these words and sentences would flash out quite naturally, so that my friends wondered at the richness of my vocabulary. I must have read parts of many books (in those early days I think I never read any book through) and a great deal of poetry in this uncomprehending way, until I discovered "Little Lord Fauntleroy," which was the first book of any consequence I read understandingly.

One day my teacher found me in a corner of the library poring over the pages of "The Scarlet Letter." I was then about eight years old. I remember she asked me if I liked little Pearl, and explained some of the words that had puzzled me. Then she told me that she had a beautiful story about a little boy which she was sure I would like better than "The Scarlet Letter." The name of the story was "Little Lord Fauntleroy," and she promised to read it to me the following summer. But we did not begin the story until August; the first few weeks of my stay at the seashore were so full of discoveries and excitement that I forgot the very existence of books. Then my teacher went to visit some friends in Boston, leaving me for a short time.

When she returned almost the first thing we did was to begin the story of "Little Lord Fauntleroy." I recall distinctly the time and place when we read the first chapters of the fascinating child's story. It was a warm afternoon in August. We were sitting together in a hammock which swung from two solemn pines at a short distance from the house. We had hurried through the dish-washing after luncheon, in order that we might have as long an afternoon as possible for the story. As we hastened through the long grass toward the hammock, the grasshoppers swarmed about us and fastened themselves on our clothes, and I remember that my teacher insisted upon picking them all off before we sat down, which seemed to me an unnecessary waste of time. The hammock was covered with pine needles, for it had not been used while my teacher was away. The warm sun shone on the pine trees and drew out all their fragrance. The air was balmy, with a tang of the sea in it. Before we began the story Miss Sullivan explained to me the things that she knew I should not understand, and as we read on she explained the unfamiliar words. At first there were many words I did not know, and the reading was constantly interrupted; but as soon as I thoroughly comprehended the situation, I became too eagerly absorbed in the story to notice mere words, and I am afraid I listened impatiently to the explanations that Miss Sullivan felt to be necessary. When her fingers were too tired to spell another word, I had for the first time a keen sense of my deprivations. I took the book in my hands and tried to feel the letters with an intensity of longing that I can never forget.

Afterward, at my eager request, Mr. Anagnos had this story embossed, and I read it again and again, until I almost knew it by heart; and all through my childhood "Little Lord Fauntleroy" was my sweet and gentle companion. I have given these details at the risk of being tedious, because they are in such vivid contrast with my vague, mutable and confused memories of earlier reading.

From "Little Lord Fauntleroy" I date the beginning of my true interest in books. During the next two years I read many books at my home and on my visits to Boston. I cannot remember what they all were, or in what order I read them; but I know that among them were "Greek Heroes," La Fontaine's "Fables," Hawthorne's "Wonder Book," "Bible Stories," Lamb's "Tales from Shakespeare," "A Child's History of England" by Dickens, "The Arabian Nights," "The Swiss Family Robinson," "The Pilgrim's Progress," "Robinson Crusoe," "Little Women," and "Heidi," a beautiful little story which I afterward read in German. I read them in the intervals between study and play with an ever-deepening sense of pleasure. I did not study nor analyze them—I did not know whether they were well written or not; I never thought about style or authorship. They laid their treasures at my feet, and I accepted them as we accept the sunshine and the love of

our friends. I loved "Little Women" because it gave me a
sense of kinship with girls and boys who could see and hear.
Circumscribed as my life was in so many ways, I had to look
between the covers of books for news of the world that lay
outside my own.

I did not care especially for "The Pilgrim's Progress,"
which I think I did not finish, or for the "Fables." I read La
Fontaine's "Fables" first in an English translation, and enjoyed them only after a half-hearted fashion. Later I read the
book again in French, and I found that, in spite of the vivid
word-pictures, and the wonderful mastery of language, I
liked it no better. I do not know why it is, but stories in which
animals are made to talk and act like human beings have
never appealed to me very strongly. The ludicrous caricatures
of the animals occupy my mind to the exclusion of the moral.

Then, again, La Fontaine seldom, if ever, appeals to our
higher moral sense. The highest chords he strikes are those of
reason and self-love. Through all the fables runs the thought
that man's morality springs wholly from self-love, and that if
that self-love is directed and restrained by reason, happiness
must follow. Now, so far as I can judge, self-love is the root of
all evil; but, of course, I may be wrong, for La Fontaine had
greater opportunities of observing men than I am likely ever
to have. I do not object so much to the cynical and satirical fables as to those in which momentous truths are taught by
monkeys and foxes.

But I love "The Jungle Book" and "Wild Animals I Have
Known." I feel a genuine interest in the animals themselves,
because they are real animals and not caricatures of men. One
sympathizes with their loves and hatreds, laughs over their
comedies, and weeps over their tragedies. And if they point a
moral, it is so subtle that we are not conscious of it.

My mind opened naturally and joyously to a conception of
antiquity. Greece, ancient Greece, exercised a mysterious fascination over me. In my fancy the pagan gods and goddesses
still walked on earth and talked face to face with men, and in
my heart I secretly built shrines to those I loved best. I knew

and loved the whole tribe of nymphs and heroes and demigods—no, not quite all, for the cruelty and greed of Medea and Jason were too monstrous to be forgiven, and I used to wonder why the gods permitted them to do wrong and then punished them for their wickedness. And the mystery is still unsolved. I often wonder how

> God can dumbness keep
> While Sin creeps grinning through His house of Time.

It was the Iliad that made Greece my paradise. I was familiar with the story of Troy before I read it in the original, and consequently I had little difficulty in making the Greek words surrender their treasures after I had passed the borderland of grammar. Great poetry, whether written in Greek or in English, needs no other interpreter than a responsive heart. Would that the host of those who make the great works of the poets odious by their analysis, impositions and laborious comments might learn this simple truth! It is not necessary that one should be able to define every word and give it its principal parts and its grammatical position in the sentence in order to understand and appreciate a fine poem. I know my learned professors have found greater riches in the Iliad than I shall ever find; but I am not avaricious. I am content that others should be wiser than I. But with all their wide and comprehensive knowledge, they cannot measure their enjoyment of that splendid epic, nor can I. When I read the finest passages of the Iliad, I am conscious of a soul-sense that lifts me above the narrow, cramping circumstances of my life. My physical limitations are forgotten—my world lies upward, the length and the breadth and the sweep of the heavens are mine!

My admiration for the Æneid is not so great, but it is none the less real. I read it as much as possible without the help of notes or dictionary, and I always like to translate the episodes that pleased me especially. The word-painting of Virgil is wonderful sometimes; but his gods and men move through the scenes of passion and strife and pity and love like the graceful figures in an Elizabethan mask, whereas in the Iliad they give three leaps and go on singing. Virgil is serene and lovely like a marble Apollo in the moonlight; Homer is a beautiful, animated youth in the full sunlight with the wind in his hair.

How easy it is to fly on paper wings! From "Greek Heroes" to the Iliad was no day's journey, nor was it altogether pleasant. One could have traveled round the world many times while I trudged my weary way through the labyrinthine mazes of grammars and dictionaries, or fell into those dreadful pitfalls called examinations, set by schools and colleges for the confusion of those who seek after knowledge. I suppose this sort of Pilgrim's Progress was justified by the end; but it seemed interminable to me, in spite of the pleasant surprises that met me now and then at a turn in the road.

I began to read the Bible long before I could understand it. Now it seems strange to me that there should have been a time when my spirit was deaf to its wondrous harmonies; but I remember well a rainy Sunday morning when, having nothing else to do, I begged my cousin to read me a story out of the Bible. Although she did not think I should understand, she began to spell into my hand the story of Joseph and his brothers. Somehow it failed to interest me. The unusual language and repetition made the story seem unreal and far away in the land of Canaan, and I fell asleep and wandered off to the land of Nod, before the brothers came with the coat of many colours unto the tent of Jacob and told their wicked lie! I cannot understand why the stories of the Greeks should have been so full of charm for me, and those of the Bible so devoid of interest, unless it was that I had made the acquaintance of several Greeks in Boston and been inspired by their enthusiasm for the stories of their country; whereas I had not met a single Hebrew or Egyptian, and therefore concluded that they were nothing more than barbarians, and the stories about them were probably all made up. Curiously enough, it never occurred to me to call Greek patronymics "queer."

But how shall I speak of the glories I have since discovered in the Bible? For years I have read it with an ever-broadening sense of joy and inspiration; and I love it as I love no other book. Still there is much in the Bible against which every instinct of my being rebels, so much that I regret the necessity which has compelled me to read it through from beginning to end. I do not think that the knowledge which I have gained of its history and sources compensates me for the unpleasant details it has forced upon my attention. For my part, I wish, with Mr. Howells, that the literature of the past might be purged of all that is ugly and barbarous in it, although I should object as much as any one to having these great works weakened or falsified.

There is something impressive, awful, in the simplicity and terrible directness of the Book of Esther. Could there be anything more dramatic than the scene in which Esther stands before her wicked lord? She knows her life is in his hands; there is no one to protect her from his wrath. Yet, conquering her woman's fear, she approaches him, animated by the noblest patriotism, having but one thought: "If I perish, I perish; but if I live, my people shall live."

The story of Ruth, too—how Oriental it is! Yet how different is the life of these simple country folks from that of the Persian capital! Ruth is so loyal and gentle-hearted, we cannot help loving her, as she stands with the reapers amid the waving corn. Her beautiful, unselfish spirit shines out like a bright star in the night of a dark and cruel age. Love like Ruth's, love which can rise above conflicting creeds and deep-seated racial prejudices, is hard to find in all the world.

The Bible gives me a deep, comforting sense that "things seen are temporal, and things unseen are eternal."

I do not remember a time since I have been capable of loving books that I have not loved Shakespeare. I cannot tell exactly when I began Lamb's "Tales from Shakespeare"; but I know that I read them at first with a child's understanding and a child's wonder. "Macbeth" seems to have impressed me most. One reading was sufficient to stamp every detail of the story upon my memory forever. For a long time the ghosts and witches pursued me even into Dreamland. I could see, absolutely see, the dagger and Lady Macbeth's little white hand—the dreadful stain was as real to me as to the grief-stricken queen.

I read "King Lear" soon after "Macbeth," and I shall never forget the feeling of horror when I came to the scene in which Gloster's eyes are put out. Anger seized me, my fingers refused to move, I sat rigid for one long moment, the blood throbbing in my temples, and all the hatred that a child can feel concentrated in my heart.

I must have made the acquaintance of Shylock and Satan about the same time, for the two characters were long associated in my mind. I remember that I was sorry for them. I felt vaguely that they could not be good even if they wished to, because no one seemed willing to help them or to give them a fair chance. Even now I cannot find it in my heart to condemn them utterly. There are moments when I feel that the Shylocks, the Judases, and even the Devil, are broken spokes in the great wheel of good which shall in due time be made whole.

It seems strange that my first reading of Shakespeare should have left me so many unpleasant memories. The bright, gentle, fanciful plays—the ones I like best now—appear not to have impressed me at first, perhaps because they reflected the habitual sunshine and gaiety of a child's life. But "there is nothing more capricious than the memory of a child: what it will hold, and what it will lose."

I have since read Shakespeare's plays many times and know parts of them by heart, but I cannot tell which of them I like best. My delight in them is as varied as my moods. The little songs and the sonnets have a meaning for me as fresh and wonderful as the dramas. But, with all my love for Shakespeare, it is often weary work to read all the meanings into his lines which critics and commentators have given them. I used to try to remember their interpretations, but they discouraged and vexed me; so I made a secret compact with myself not to try any more. This compact I have only just broken in my study of Shakespeare under Professor Kittredge. I know there are many things in Shakespeare, and in the world, that I do not understand; and I am glad to see veil after veil lift gradually, revealing new realms of thought and beauty.

Next to poetry I love history. I have read every historical work that I have been able to lay my hands on, from a catalogue of dry facts and dryer dates to Green's impartial, picturesque "History of the English People"; from Freeman's "History of Europe" to Emerton's "Middle Ages." The first book that gave me any real sense of the value of history was Swinton's "World's History," which I received on my thirteenth birthday. Though I believe it is no longer considered valid, yet I have kept it ever since as one of my treasures. From it I learned how the races of men spread from land to land and built great cities, how a few great rulers, earthly Titans, put everything under their feet, and with a decisive word opened the gates of happiness for millions and closed them upon millions more; how different nations pioneered in art and knowledge and broke ground for the mightier growths of coming ages; how civilization underwent, as it were, the holocaust of a degenerate age, and rose again, like the Phoenix, among the nobler sons of the North; and how by liberty, tolerance and education the great and the wise have opened the way for the salvation of the whole world.

In my college reading I have become somewhat familiar with French and German literature. The German puts strength before beauty, and truth before convention, both in life and literature. There is a vehement, sledge-hammer vigour about everything that he does. When he speaks, it is not to impress others, but because his heart would burst if he did not find an outlet for the thoughts that burn in his soul.

Then, too, there is in German literature a fine reserve which I like; but its chief glory is the recognition I find in it of the redeeming potency of woman's self-sacrificing love. This thought pervades all German literature and is mystically expressed in Goethe's "Faust":

All things transitory
  But as symbols are sent.
Earth's insufficiency
  Here grows to event.
The indescribable
Here it is done.
The Woman Soul leads us upward and on!

Of all the French writers that I have read, I like Molière and Racine best. There are fine things in Balzac and passages in Mérimée which strike one like a keen blast of sea air. Alfred de Musset is impossible! I admire Victor Hugo—I appreciate his genius, his brilliancy, his romanticism; though he is not one of my literary passions. But Hugo and Goethe and Schiller and all great poets of all great nations are interpreters of eternal things, and my spirit reverently follows them into the regions where Beauty and Truth and Goodness are one.

I am afraid I have written too much about my book-friends, and yet I have mentioned only the authors I love most; and from this fact one might easily suppose that my circle of friends was very limited and undemocratic, which would be a very wrong impression. I like many writers for many reasons—Carlyle for his ruggedness and scorn of shams; Wordsworth, who teaches the oneness of man and nature; I find an exquisite pleasure in the oddities and surprises of Hood, in Herrick's quaintness and the palpable scent of lily and rose in his verses; I like Whittier for his enthusiasms and moral rectitude. I knew him, and the gentle remembrance of our friendship doubles the pleasure I have in reading his poems. I love Mark Twain—who does not? The gods, too, loved him and put into his heart all manner of wisdom; then, fearing lest he should become a pessimist, they spanned his mind with a rainbow of love and faith. I like Scott for his freshness, dash and large honesty. I love all writers whose minds, like Lowell's, bubble up in the sunshine of optimism—fountains of joy and good will, with occasionally a splash of anger and here and there a healing spray of sympathy and pity.

In a word, literature is my Utopia. Here I am not disfranchised. No barrier of the senses shuts me out from the sweet, gracious discourse of my book-friends. They talk to me without embarrassment or awkwardness. The things I have learned and the things I have been taught seem of ridiculously little importance compared with their "large loves and heavenly charities."

CHAPTER 22

I TRUST THAT my readers have not concluded from the preceding chapter on books that reading is my only pleasure; my pleasures and amusements are many and varied.

More than once in the course of my story I have referred to my love of the country and out-of-door sports. When I was quite a little girl, I learned to row and swim, and during the summer, when I am at Wrentham, Massachusetts, I almost live in my boat. Nothing gives me greater pleasure than to take my friends out rowing when they come to visit me. Of course, I cannot guide the boat very well. Some one usually sits in the stern and manages the rudder while I row. Sometimes, however, I go rowing without the rudder. It is fun to try to steer by the scent of water-grasses and lilies, and of bushes that grow on the shore. I use oars with leather bands, which keep them in position in the oarlocks, and I know by the resistance of the water when the oars are evenly poised. In the same manner I can also tell when I am pulling against the current. I like to contend with wind and wave. What is more exhilarating than to make your staunch little boat, obedient to your will and muscle, go skimming lightly over glistening, tilting waves, and to feel the steady, imperious surge of the water!

I also enjoy canoeing, and I suppose you will smile when I

say that I especially like it on moonlight nights. I cannot, it is true, see the moon climb up the sky behind the pines and steal softly across the heavens, making a shining path for us to follow; but I know she is there, and as I lie back among the pillows and put my hand in the water, I fancy that I feel the shimmer of her garments as she passes. Sometimes a daring little fish slips betweeen my fingers, and often a pond-lily presses shyly against my hand. Frequently, as we emerge from the shelter of a cove or inlet, I am suddenly conscious of the spaciousness of the air about me. A luminous warmth seems to enfold me. Whether it comes from the trees which have been heated by the sun, or from the water, I can never discover. I have had the same strange sensation even in the heart of the city. I have felt it on cold, stormy days and at night. It is like the kiss of warm lips on my face.

My favourite amusement is sailing. In the summer of 1901 I visited Nova Scotia, and had opportunities such as I had not enjoyed before to make the acquaintance of the ocean. After spending a few days in Evangeline's country, about which Longfellow's beautiful poem has woven a spell of enchantment, Miss Sullivan and I went to Halifax, where we remained the greater part of the summer. The harbour was our joy, our paradise. What glorious sails we had to Bedford Basin, to McNabb's Island, to York Redoubt, and to the Northwest Arm! And at night what soothing, wondrous hours we spent in the shadow of the great, silent men-of-war. Oh, it was all so interesting, so beautiful! The memory of it is a joy forever.

One day we had a thrilling experience. There was a regatta in the Northwest Arm, in which the boats from the different warships were engaged. We went in a sail-boat along with many others to watch the races. Hundreds of little sail-boats swung to and fro close by, and the sea was calm. When the races were over, and we turned our faces homeward, one of the party noticed a black cloud drifting in from the sea, which grew and spread and thickened until it covered the whole sky. The wind rose, and the waves chopped angrily at unseen barriers. Our little boat confronted the gale fearlessly; with sails spread and ropes taut, she seemed to sit upon the wind. Now she swirled in the billows, now she sprang upward on a gigantic wave, only to be driven down with angry howl and hiss. Down came the mainsail. Tacking and jibbing, we wrestled with opposing winds that drove us from side to side with impetuous fury. Our hearts beat fast, and our hands trembled with excitement, not fear; for we had the hearts of vikings, and we knew that our skipper was master of the situation. He had steered through many a storm with firm hand and sea-wise eye. As they passed us, the large craft and the gunboats in the harbour saluted and the seamen shouted applause for the master of the only little sail-boat that ventured out into the storm. At last, cold, hungry and weary, we reached our pier.

Last summer I spent in one of the loveliest nooks of one of the most charming villages in New England. Wrentham, Massachusetts, is associated with nearly all of my joys and sorrows. For many years Red Farm, by King Philip's Pond, the home of Mr. J. E. Chamberlin and his family, was my home. I remember with deepest gratitude the kindness of these dear friends and the happy days I spent with them. The sweet companionship of their children meant much to me. I joined in all their sports and rambles through the woods and frolics in the water. The prattle of the little ones and their pleasure in the stories I told them of elf and gnome, of hero and wily bear, are pleasant things to remember. Mr. Chamberlin initiated me into the mysteries of tree and wild-flower, until with the little ear of love I heard the flow of sap in the oak, and saw the sun glint from leaf to leaf. Thus it is that

> *Even as the roots, shut in the darksome earth,*
> *Share in the tree-top's joyance, and conceive*
> *Of sunshine and wide air and wingéd things,*
> *By sympathy of nature, so do I*

gave evidence of things unseen.

It seems to me that there is in each of us a capacity to

comprehend the impressions and emotions which have been experienced by mankind from the beginning. Each individual has a subconscious memory of the green earth and murmuring waters, and blindness and deafness cannot rob him of this gift from past generations. This inherited capacity is a sort of sixth sense—a soul-sense which sees, hears, feels, all in one.

I have many tree friends in Wrentham. One of them, a splendid oak, is the special pride of my heart. I take all my other friends to see this king-tree. It stands on a bluff overlooking King Philip's Pond, and those who are wise in tree lore say it must have stood there eight hundred or a thousand years. There is a tradition that under this tree King Philip, the heroic Indian chief, gazed his last on earth and sky.

I had another tree friend, gentle and more approachable than the great oak—a linden that grew in the dooryard at Red Farm. One afternoon, during a terrible thunderstorm, I felt a tremendous crash against the side of the house and knew, even before they told me, that the linden had fallen. We went out to see the hero that had withstood so many tempests, and it wrung my heart to see him prostrate who had mightily striven and was now mightily fallen.

But I must not forget that I was going to write about last summer in particular. As soon as my examinations were over, Miss Sullivan and I hastened to this green nook, where we have a little cottage on one of the three lakes for which Wrentham is famous. Here the long, sunny days were mine, and all thoughts of work and college and the noisy city were thrust into the background. In Wrentham we caught echoes of what was happening in the world—war, alliance, social conflict. We heard of the cruel, unnecessary fighting in the far-away Pacific, and learned of the struggles going on between capital and labour. We knew that beyond the border of our Eden men were making history by the sweat of their brows when they might better make a holiday. But we little heeded these things. These things would pass away; here were lakes and woods and broad daisy-starred fields and sweet-breathed meadows, and they shall endure forever.

People who think that all sensations reach us through the eye and the ear have expressed surprise that I should notice any difference, except possibly the absence of pavements, between walking in city streets and in country roads. They forget that my whole body is alive to the conditions about me. The rumble and roar of the city smite the nerves of my face, and I feel the ceaseless tramp of an unseen multitude, and the dissonant tumult frets my spirit. The grinding of heavy wagons on hard pavements and the monotonous clangour of machinery are all the more torturing to the nerves if one's attention is not diverted by the panorama that is always present in the noisy streets to people who can see.

In the country one sees only Nature's fair works, and one's soul is not saddened by the cruel struggle for mere existence that goes on in the crowded city. Several times I have visited the narrow, dirty streets where the poor live, and I grow hot and indignant to think that good people should be content to live in fine houses and become strong and beautiful, while others are condemned to live in hideous, sunless tenements and grow ugly, withered and cringing. The children who crowd these grimy alleys, half-clad and underfed, shrink away from your outstretched hand as if from a blow. Dear little creatures, they crouch in my heart and haunt me with a constant sense of pain. There are men and women, too, all gnarled and bent out of shape. I have felt their hard, rough hands and realized what an endless struggle their existence must be—no more than a series of scrimmages, thwarted attempts to do something. Their life seems an immense disparity between effort and opportunity. The sun and the air are God's free gifts to all, we say; but are they so? In yonder city's dingy alleys the sun shines not, and the air is foul. Oh, man, how dost thou forget and obstruct thy brother man, and say, "Give us this day our daily bread," when he has none! Oh, would that men would leave the city, its splendour and its tumult and its gold, and return to wood and field and simple, honest living! Then would their children grow stately as noble trees, and their thoughts sweet and pure as wayside flowers. It is impossible not to think of all this when I return to the country after a year of work in town.

What a joy it is to feel the soft, springy earth under my feet once more, to follow grassy roads that lead to ferny brooks where I can bathe my fingers in a cataract of rippling notes, or to clamber over a stone wall into green fields that tumble and roll and climb in riotous gladness!

Next to a leisurely walk I enjoy a "spin" on my tandem bicycle. It is splendid to feel the wind blowing in my face and the springy motion of my iron steed. The rapid rush through the air gives me a delicious sense of strength and buoyancy, and the exercise makes my pulses dance and my heart sing.

Whenever it is possible, my dog accompanies me on a walk or ride or sail. I have had many dog friends—huge mastiffs, soft-eyed spaniels, wood-wise setters and honest, homely bull terriers. At present the lord of my affections is one of these bull terriers. He has a long pedigree, a crooked tail and the drollest "phiz" in dogdom. My dog friends seem to understand my limitations, and always keep close beside me when I am alone. I love their affectionate ways and the eloquent wag of their tails.

When a rainy day keeps me indoors, I amuse myself after the manner of other girls. I like to knit and crochet; I read in the happy-go-lucky way I love, here and there a line; or perhaps I play a game or two of checkers or chess with a friend. I have a special board on which I play these games. The squares are cut out, so that the men stand in them firmly. The black checkers are flat and the white ones curved on top. Each checker has a hole in the middle in which a brass knob can be placed to distinguish the king from the commons. The chessmen are of two sizes, the white larger than the black, so that I have no trouble in following my opponent's maneuvers by moving my hands lightly over the board after a play. The jar made by shifting the men from one hole to another tells me when it is my turn.

If I happen to be all alone and in an idle mood, I play a game of solitaire, of which I am very fond. I use playing cards marked in the upper right-hand corner with braille symbols which indicate the value of the card.

If there are children around, nothing pleases me so much as to frolic with them. I find even the smallest child excellent company, and I am glad to say that children usually like me. They lead me about and show me the things they are interested in. Of course the little ones cannot spell on their fingers; but I manage to read their lips. If I do not succeed they resort to dumb show. Sometimes I make a mistake and do the wrong thing. A burst of childish laughter greets my blunder, and the pantomime begins all over again. I often tell them stories or teach them a game, and the winged hours depart and leave us good and happy.

Museums and art stores are also sources of pleasure and inspiration. Doubtless it will seem strange to many that the hand unaided by sight can feel action, sentiment, beauty in the cold marble; and yet it is true that I derive genuine pleasure from touching great works of art. As my finger tips trace line and curve, they discover the thought and emotion which the artist has portrayed. I can feel in the faces of gods and heroes hate, courage and love, just as I can detect them in living faces I am permitted to touch. I feel in Diana's posture the grace and freedom of the forest and the spirit that tames the mountain lion and subdues the fiercest passions. My soul delights in the repose and gracious curves of the Venus; and in Barré's bronzes the secrets of the jungle are revealed to me.

A medallion of Homer hangs on the wall of my study, conveniently low, so that I can easily reach it and touch the beautiful, sad face with loving reverence. How well I know each line in that majestic brow—tracks of life and bitter evidence of struggle and sorrow; those sightless eyes seeking, even in the cold plaster, for the light and the blue skies of his beloved Hellas, but seeking in vain; that beautiful mouth, firm and true and tender. It is the face of a poet, and of a man acquainted with sorrow. Ah, how well I understand his deprivation—the perpetual night in which he dwelt—

O dark, dark, amid the blaze of noon,
Irrecoverably dark, total eclipse
Without all hope of day!

In imagination I can hear Homer singing, as with unsteady, hesitating steps he gropes his way from camp to camp— singing of life, of love, of war, of the splendid achievements of a noble race. It was a wonderful, glorious song, and it won the blind poet an immortal crown, the admiration of all ages.

I sometimes wonder if the hand is not more sensitive to the beauties of sculpture than the eye. I should think the wonderful rhythmical flow of lines and curves could be more subtly felt than seen. Be this as it may, I know that I can feel the heartthrobs of the ancient Greeks in their marble gods and goddesses.

Another pleasure, which comes more rarely than the others, is going to the theatre. I enjoy having a play described to me while it is being acted on the stage far more than reading it, because then it seems as if I were living in the midst of stirring events. It has been my privilege to meet a few great actors and actresses who have the power of so bewitching you that you forget time and place and live again in the romantic past. I have been permitted to touch the face and costume of Miss Ellen Terry as she impersonated our ideal of a queen; and there was about her that divinity that hedges sublimest woe. Beside her stood Sir Henry Irving, wearing the symbols of kingship; and there was majesty of intellect in his every gesture and attitude and the royalty that subdues and overcomes in every line of his sensitive face. In the king's face, which he wore as a mask, there was a remoteness and inaccessibility of grief which I shall never forget.

I also know Mr. Jefferson. I am proud to count him among my friends. I go to see him whenever I happen to be where he is acting. The first time I saw him act was while at school in New York. He played "Rip Van Winkle." I had often read the story, but I had never felt the charm of Rip's slow, quaint, kind ways as I did in the play. Mr. Jefferson's beautiful, pathetic representation quite carried me away with delight. I have a picture of old Rip in my fingers which they will never lose. After the play Miss Sullivan took me to see him behind the scenes, and I felt of his curious garb and his flowing hair and beard. Mr. Jefferson let me touch his face so that I could imagine how he looked on waking from that strange sleep of twenty years, and he showed me how poor old Rip staggered to his feet.

I have also seen him in "The Rivals." Once while I was calling on him in Boston he acted the most striking parts of "The Rivals" for me. The reception-room where we sat served for a stage. He and his son seated themselves at the big table, and Bob Acres wrote his challenge. I followed all his movements with my hands, and caught the drollery of his blunders and gestures in a way that would have been impossible had it all been spelled to me. Then they rose to fight the duel, and I followed the swift thrusts and parries of the swords and the waverings of poor Bob as his courage oozed out at his finger ends. Then the great actor gave his coat a hitch and his mouth a twitch, and in an instance I was in the village of Falling Water and felt Schneider's shaggy head against my knee. Mr. Jefferson recited the best dialogues of "Rip Van Winkle," in which the tear came close upon the smile. He asked me to indicate as far as I could the gestures and action that should go with the lines. Of course, I have no sense whatever of dramatic action, and could make only random guesses; but with masterful art he suited the action to the word. The sigh of Rip as he murmurs, "Is a man so soon forgotten when he is gone?" the dismay with which he searches for dog and gun after his long sleep, and his comical irresolution over signing the contract with Derrick—all these seem to be right out of life itself; that is, the ideal life, where things happen as we think they should.

I remember well the first time I went to the theatre. It was twelve years ago. Elsie Leslie, the little actress, was in Boston, and Miss Sullivan took me to see her in "The Prince and the Pauper." I shall never forget the ripple of alternating joy and woe that ran through that beautiful little play, or the wonderful child who acted it. After the play I was permitted to go behind the scenes and meet her in her royal costume. It would have been hard to find a lovelier or more lovable child than Elsie, as she stood with a cloud of golden hair floating over her shoulders, smiling brightly, showing no signs of shyness or fatigue, though she had been playing to an immense audience. I was only just learning to speak, and had previously repeated her name until I could say it perfectly. Imagine my delight when she understood the few words I spoke to her and without hesitation stretched her hand to greet me.

Is it not true, then, that my life with all its limitations touches at many points the life of the World Beautiful? Everything has its wonders, even darkness and silence, and I learn, whatever state I may be in, therein to be content.

Sometimes, it is true, a sense of isolation enfolds me like a cold mist as I sit alone and wait at life's shut gate. Beyond there is light, and music, and sweet companionship; but I may not enter. Fate, silent, pitiless, bars the way. Fain would I question his imperious decree; for my heart is still undisciplined and passionate; but my tongue will not utter the bitter, futile words that rise to my lips, and they fall back into my heart like unshed tears. Silence sits immense upon my soul. Then comes hope with a smile and whispers, "There is joy in self-forgetfulness." So I try to make the light in others' eyes my sun, the music in others' ears my symphony, the smile on others' lips my happiness.

CHAPTER 23

WOULD THAT I could enrich this sketch with the names of all those who have ministered to my happiness! Some of them would be found written in our literature and dear to the hearts of many, while others would be wholly unknown to most of my readers. But their influence, though it escapes fame, shall live immortal in the lives that have been sweetened and ennobled by it. Those are red-letter days in our lives when we meet people who thrill us like a fine poem, people whose handshake is brimful of unspoken sympathy, and whose sweet, rich natures impart to our eager, impatient spirits a wonderful restfulness which, in its essence, is divine. The perplexities, irritations and worries that have absorbed us pass like unpleasant dreams, and we wake to see with new eyes and hear with new ears the beauty and harmony of God's real world. The solemn nothings that fill our everyday life blossom suddenly into bright possibilities. In a word, while such friends are near us we feel that all is well. Perhaps we never saw them before, and they may never cross our life's path again; but the influence of their calm, mellow natures is a libation poured upon our discontent, and we feel its healing touch, as the ocean feels the mountain stream freshening its brine.

I have often been asked, "Do not people bore you?" I do not understand quite what that means. I suppose the calls of the stupid and curious, especially of newspaper reporters, are always inopportune. I also dislike people who try to talk down to my understanding. They are like people who when walking with you try to shorten their steps to suit yours; the hypocrisy in both cases is equally exasperating.

The hands of those I meet are dumbly eloquent to me. The touch of some hands is an impertinence. I have met people so empty of joy, that when I clasped their frosty finger tips, it seemed as if I were shaking hands with a northeast storm. Others there are whose hands have sunbeams in them, so that their grasp warms my heart. It may be only the clinging touch of a child's hand; but there is as much potential sunshine in it for me as there is in a loving glance for others. A hearty handshake or a friendly letter gives me genuine pleasure.

I have many far-off friends whom I have never seen. Indeed they are so many that I have often been unable to reply to their letters; but I wish to say here that I am always grateful for their kind words, however insufficiently I acknowledge them.

I count it one of the sweetest privileges of my life to have known and conversed with many men of genius. Only those who knew Bishop Brooks can appreciate the joy his friendship was to those who possessed it. As a child I loved to sit on his knee and clasp his great hand with one of mine, while Miss Sullivan spelled into the other his beautiful words about God and the spiritual world. I heard him with a child's wonder and delight. My spirit could not reach up to his, but he gave me a real sense of joy in life, and I never left him without carrying away a fine thought that grew in beauty and depth of meaning as I grew. Once, when I was puzzled to know why there were so many religions, he said: "There is one universal religion, Helen—the religion of love. Love your Heavenly Father with your whole heart and soul, love every child of God as much as ever you can, and remember that the possibilities of good are greater than the possibilities of evil; and you have the key to Heaven." And his life was a happy illustration of his great truth. In his noble soul love and widest knowledge were blended with faith that had become insight. He saw

God in all that liberates and lifts,
In all that humbles, sweetens and consoles.

Bishop Brooks taught me no special creed or dogma; but he impressed upon my mind two great ideas—the fatherhood of God and the brotherhood of man, and made me feel that these truths underlie all creeds and forms of worship. God is love, God is our Father, and we are His children; therefore the darkest clouds will break, and though right be worsted, wrong shall not triumph.

I am too happy in this world to think much about the future, except to remember that I have cherished friends awaiting me there in God's beautiful Somewhere. In spite of the lapse of years, they seem so close to me that I should not think it strange if at any moment they should clasp my hand and speak words of endearment as they used to before they went away.

Since Bishop Brooks died I have read the Bible through; also some philosophical works on religion, among them Swedenborg's "Heaven and Hell" and Drummond's "Ascent of Man," and I have found no creed or system more soul-satisfying than Bishop Brooks's creed of love. I knew Mr. Henry Drummond, and the memory of his strong, warm hand-clasp is like a benediction. He was the most sympathetic of companions. He knew so much and was so genial that it was impossible to feel dull in his presence.

I remember well the first time I saw Dr. Oliver Wendell Holmes. He had invited Miss Sullivan and me to call on him one Sunday afternoon. It was early in the spring, just after I had learned to speak. We were shown at once to his library where we found him seated in a big armchair by an open fire which glowed and crackled on the hearth, thinking, he said, of other days.

"And listening to the murmur of the River Charles," I suggested.

"Yes," he replied, "the Charles has many dear associations for me." There was an odour of print and leather in the room which told me that it was full of books, and I stretched out my hand instinctively to find them. My fingers lighted upon a beautiful volume of Tennyson's poems, and when Miss Sullivan told me what it was I began to recite:

Break, break, break
On thy cold gray stones, O sea!

But I stopped suddenly. I felt tears on my hand. I had made my beloved poet weep, and I was greatly distressed. He made me sit in his armchair, while he brought different interesting things for me to examine, and at his request I recited "The Chambered Nautilus," which was then my favourite poem. After that I saw Dr. Holmes many times and learned to love the man as well as the poet.

One beautiful summer day, not long after my meeting with Dr. Holmes, Miss Sullivan and I visited Whittier in his quiet home on the Merrimac. His gentle courtesy and quaint speech won my heart. He had a book of his poems in raised print from which I read "In School Days." He was delighted that I could pronounce the words so well, and said that he had no difficulty in understanding me. Then I asked many questions about the poem, and read his answers by placing my fingers on his lips. He said he was the little boy in the poem, and that the girl's name was Sally, and more which I have forgotten. I also recited "Laus Deo," and as I spoke the concluding verses, he placed in my hands a statue of a slave from whose crouching figure the fetters were falling, even as they fell from Peter's limbs when the angel led him forth out of prison. Afterward we went into his study, and he wrote his* autograph for my teacher and expressed his admiration of her work, saying to me, "She is thy spiritual liberator." Then he led me to the gate and kissed me tenderly on my forehead. I promised to visit him again the following summer; but he died before the promise was fulfilled.

Dr. Edward Everett Hale is one of my very oldest friends. I have known him since I was eight, and my love for him has increased with my years. His wise, tender sympathy has been the support of Miss Sullivan and me in times of trial and sorrow, and his strong hand has helped us over many rough

---

*"With great admiration of thy noble work in releasing from bondage the mind of thy dear pupil, I am truly thy friend. John G. Whittier."

places; and what he has done for us he has done for thousands of those who have difficult tasks to accomplish. He has filled the old skins of dogma with the new wine of love, and shown men what it is to believe, live and be free. What he has taught we have seen beautifully expressed in his own life—love of country, kindness to the least of his brethren, and a sincere desire to live upward and onward. He has been a prophet and an inspirer of men, and a mighty doer of the Word, the friend of all his race—God bless him!

I have already written of my first meeting with Dr. Alexander Graham Bell. Since then I have spent many happy days with him at Washington and at his beautiful home in the heart of Cape Breton Island, near Baddeck, the village made famous by Charles Dudley Warner's book. Here in Dr. Bell's laboratory, or in the fields on the shore of the great Bras d'Or, I have spent many delightful hours listening to what he had to tell me about his experiments, and helping him fly kites by means of which he expects to discover the laws that shall govern the future airship. Dr. Bell is proficient in many fields of science, and has the art of making every subject he touches interesting, even the most abstruse theories. He makes you feel that if you only had a little more time, you, too, might be an inventor. He has a humorous and poetic side, too. His dominating passion is his love for children. He is never quite so happy as when he has a little deaf child in his arms. His labours in behalf of the deaf will live on and bless generations of children yet to come; and we love him alike for what he himself has achieved and for what he has evoked from others.

During the two years I spent in New York I had many opportunities to talk with distinguished people whose names I had often heard, but whom I had never expected to meet. Most of them I met first in the house of my good friend, Mr. Laurence Hutton. It was a great privilege to visit him and dear Mrs. Hutton in their lovely home, and see their library and read the beautiful sentiments and bright thoughts gifted friends had written for them. It has been truly said that Mr.

Hutton has the faculty of bringing out in every one the best thoughts and kindest sentiments. One does not need to read "A Boy I Knew" to understand him—the most generous, sweet-natured boy I ever knew, a good friend in all sorts of weather, who traces the footprints of love in the life of dogs as well as in that of his fellow-men.

Mrs. Hutton is a true and tried friend. Much that I hold sweetest, much that I hold most precious, I owe to her. She had oftenest advised and helped me in my progress through college. When I find my work particularly difficult and discouraging, she writes me letters that make me feel glad and brave; for she is one of those from whom we learn that one painful duty fulfilled makes the next plainer and easier.

Mr. Hutton introduced me to many of his literary friends, greatest of whom are Mr. William Dean Howells and Mark Twain. I also met Mr. Richard Watson Gilder and Mr. Edmund Clarence Stedman. I also knew Mr. Charles Dudley Warner, the most delightful of story-tellers and the most beloved friend, whose sympathy was so broad that it may be truly said of him, he loved all living things and his neighbour as himself. Once Mr. Warner brought to see me the dear poet of the woodlands—Mr. John Burroughs. They were all gentle and sympathetic and I felt the charm of their manner as much as I had felt the brilliancy of their essays and poems. I could not keep pace with all these literary folk as they glanced from subject to subject and entered into deep dispute, or made conversation sparkle with epigrams and happy witticisms. I was like little Ascanius, who followed with unequal steps the heroic strides of Æneas on his march toward mighty destinies. But they spoke many gracious words to me. Mr. Gilder told me about his moonlight journeys across the vast desert to the Pyramids, and in a letter he wrote me he made his mark under his signature deep in the paper so that I could feel it. This reminds me that Dr. Hale used to give a personal touch to his letters to me by pricking his signature in Braille. I read from Mark Twain's lips one or two of his good stories. He has his own way of thinking, saying and doing everything. I feel the twinkle of his eye in his handshake. Even while he utters his cynical wisdom in an indescribably droll voice, he makes you feel that his heart is a tender Iliad of human sympathy.

There are a host of other interesting people I met in New York: Mrs. Mary Mapes Dodge, the beloved editor of *St. Nicholas,* and Mrs. Riggs (Kate Douglas Wiggin), the sweet author of "Patsy." I received from them gifts that have the gentle concurrence of the heart, books containing their own thoughts, soul-illumined letters, and photographs that I love to have described again and again. But there is not space to mention all my friends, and indeed there are things about them hidden behind the wings of cherubim, things too sacred to set forth in cold print. It is with hesitancy that I have spoken even of Mrs. Laurence Hutton.

I shall mention only two other friends. One is Mrs. William Thaw, of Pittsburgh, whom I have often visited in her home, Lyndhurst. She is always doing something to make some one happy, and her generosity and wise counsel have never failed my teacher and me in all the years we have known her.

To the other friend I am also deeply indebted. He is well known for the powerful hand with which he guides vast enterprises, and his wonderful abilities have gained for him the respect of all. Kind to every one, he goes about doing good, silent and unseen. Again I touch upon the circle of honoured names I must not mention; but I would fain acknowledge his generosity and affectionate interest which make it possible for me to go to college.

Thus it is that my friends have made the story of my life. In a thousand ways they have turned my limitations into beautiful privileges, and enabled me to walk serene and happy in the shadow cast by my deprivation.

LETTERS

(1887–1901)

INTRODUCTION FROM THE 1903 DOUBLEDAY EDITION

John Albert Macy

HELEN KELLER'S letters are important, not only as a supplementary story of her life, but as a demonstration of her growth in thought and expression—the growth which in itself has made her distinguished.

These letters are, however, not merely remarkable as the productions of a deaf and blind girl, to be read with wonder and curiosity; they are good letters almost from the first. The best passages are those in which she talks about herself, and gives her world in terms of her experience of it. Her views on the precession of the equinoxes are not important, but most important are her accounts of what speech meant to her, of how she felt the statues, the dogs, the chickens at the poultry show, and how she stood in the aisle of St. Bartholomew's and felt the organ rumble. Those are passages of which one would ask for more. The reason they are comparatively few is that all her life she has been trying to be "like other people," and so she too often describes things not as they appear to her, but as they appear to one with eyes and ears.

One cause for the excellence of her letters is the great number of them. They are the exercises which have trained her to write. She has lived at different times in different parts of the country, and so has been separated from most of her friends and relatives. Of her friends, many have been distinguished people, to whom—not often, I think, at the sacrifice of spontaneity—she has felt it necessary to write well. To them and to a few friends with whom she is in closest sympathy she writes with intimate frankness whatever she is thinking about. Her naïve retelling of a child's tale she has heard, like the story of

"Little Jakey," which she rehearses for Dr. Holmes and Bishop Brooks, is charming and her grave paraphrase of the day's lesson in geography or botany, her parrot-like repetition of what she has heard, and her conscious display of new words, are delightful and instructive; for they show not only what she was learning, but how, by putting it all into letters, she made the new knowledge and the new words her own.

So these selections from Miss Keller's correspondence are made with two purposes—to show her development and to preserve the most entertaining and significant passages from several hundred letters. Many of those written before 1892 were published in the reports of the Perkins Institution for the Blind. All letters up to that year are printed intact, for it is legitimate to be interested in the degree of skill the child showed in writing, even to details of punctuation; so it is well to preserve a literal integrity of reproduction. From the letters after the year 1892 I have culled in the spirit of one making an anthology, choosing the passages best in style and most important from the point of view of biography. Where I have been able to collate the original letters I have preserved everything as Miss Keller wrote it, punctuation, spelling, and all. I have done nothing but select and cut.

The letters are arranged in chronological order. One or two letters from Bishop Brooks, Dr. Holmes, and Whittier are put immediately after the letters to which they are replies. Except for two or three important letters of 1901, these selections cease with the year 1900. In that year Miss Keller entered college. Now that she is a grown woman, her mature letters should be judged like those of any other person, and it seems best that no more of her correspondence be published unless she should become distinguished beyond the fact that she is the only well-educated deaf and blind person in the world.

LETTERS

(1887–1901)

M ISS SULLIVAN began to teach Helen Keller on March 3rd, 1887. Three months and a half after the first word was spelled into her hand, she wrote in pencil this letter.

TO HER COUSIN ANNA
(MRS. GEORGE T. TURNER)

(*Tuscumbia, Alabama, June 17, 1887.*)

helen write anna george will give helen apple simpson
will shoot bird jack will give helen stick of candy
doctor will give mildred medicine mother will make
mildred new dress

(NO SIGNATURE)

Twenty-five days later, while she was on a short visit away from home, she wrote to her mother. Two words are almost illegible, and the angular print slants in every direction.

TO MRS. KATE ADAMS KELLER

(*Huntsville, Alabama, July 12, 1887.*)

Helen will write mother letter papa did give helen
medicine mildred will sit in swing mildred did kiss
helen teacher did give helen peach george is sick in

bed george arm is hurt anna did give helen lemonade dog did stand up.

conductor did punch ticket papa did give helen drink of water in car

carlotta did give helen flowers anna will buy helen pretty new hat helen will hug and kiss mother helen will come home grandmother does love helen

good-by
(NO SIGNATURE.)

By the following September Helen shows improvement in fullness of construction and more extended relations of thought.

TO THE BLIND GIRLS AT THE PERKINS INSTITUTION IN SOUTH BOSTON

(*Tuscumbia, September, 1887.*)

Helen will write little blind girls a letter Helen and teacher will come to see little blind girls Helen and teacher will go in steam car to boston Helen and blind girls will have fun blind girls can talk on fingers Helen will see Mr. anagnos Mr. anagnos will love and kiss Helen Helen will go to school with blind girls Helen can read and count and spell and write like blind girls mildred will not go to bostom Mildred does cry prince and jumbo will not go to boston papa does shoot ducks with gun and ducks do fall in water and jumbo and mamie do swim in water and bring ducks out in mouth to papa Helen does play with dogs Helen does ride on horseback with teacher Helen does give handee grass in hand teacher does whip handee to go fast Helen is blind Helen will put letter in envelope for blind girls

good-by
HELEN KELLER

A few weeks later her style is more nearly correct and freer in movement. She improves in idiom, although she still omits articles and uses the "did" construction for the simple past. This is an idiom common among children.

TO THE BLIND GIRLS AT THE PERKINS INSTITUTION

(Tuscumbia, October 24, 1887.)

dear little blind girls
I will write you a letter I thank you for pretty desk I did write to mother in memphis on it mother and mildred came home wednesday mother brought me a pretty new dress and hat papa did go to huntsville he brought me apples and candy I and teacher will come to boston and see you nancy is my doll she does cry I do rock nancy to sleep mildred is sick doctor will give her medicine to make her well. I and teacher did go to church sunday mr. lane did read in book and talk Lady did play organ. I did give man money in basket. I will be good girl and teacher will curl my hair lovely. I will hug and kiss little blind girls mr. anagnos will come to see me.

good-by
HELEN KELLER

TO MR. MICHAEL ANAGNOS, DIRECTOR OF THE PERKINS INSTITUTION

(Tuscumbia, November, 1887.)

dear mr. anagnos I will write you a letter. I and teacher did have pictures. teacher will send it to you. photographer does make pictures. carpenter does build new houses. gardener does dig and hoe ground and plant vegetables. my doll nancy is sleeping. she is sick. mildred is well uncle frank has gone hunting deer. we

will have venison for breakfast when he comes home. I
did ride in wheel barrow and teacher did push it.
simpson did give me popcorn and walnuts. cousin rosa
has gone to see her mother. people do go to church
sunday. I did read in my book about fox and box. fox
can sit in the box. I do like to read in my book. you do
love me. I do love you.

good-by
HELEN KELLER

TO DR. ALEXANDER GRAHAM BELL

(*Tuscumbia, November, 1887.*)

DEAR MR. BELL.
I am glad to write you a letter. Father will send you
picture. I and Father and aunt did go to see you in
Washington. I did play with your watch. I do love you.
I saw doctor in Washington. He looked at my eyes. I
can read stories in my book. I can write and spell and
count. good girl. My sister can walk and run. We do
have fun with Jumbo. Prince is not good dog. He can
not get birds. Rat did kill baby pigeons. I am sorry. Rat
does not know wrong. I and mother and teacher will go
to Boston in June. I will see little blind girls. Nancy
will go with me. She is a good doll. Father will buy me
lovely new watch. Cousin Anna gave me a pretty doll.
Her name is Allie.

Good-by,
HELEN KELLER.

By the beginning of the next year her idioms are firmer. More
adjectives appear, including adjectives of colour. Although
she can have no sensuous knowledge of colour, she can use
the words, as we use most of our vocabulary, intellectually,
with truth, not to impression, but to fact. This letter is to a
schoolmate at the Perkins Institution.

TO MISS SARAH TOMLINSON

Tuscumbia, Ala. Jan. 2nd 1888.

Dear Sarah

I am happy to write to you this morning. I hope
Mr. Anagnos is coming to see me soon. I will go to
Boston in June and I will buy father gloves, and James
nice collar, and Simpson cuffs. I saw Miss Betty and
her scholars. They had a pretty Christmas tree, and
there were many pretty presents on it for little
children. I had a mug, and little bird and candy. I had
many lovely things for Christmas. Aunt gave me a
trunk for Nancy and clothes. I went to party with
teacher and mother. We did dance and play and eat
nuts and candy and cakes and oranges and I did
have fun with little boys and girls. Mrs. Hopkins did
send me lovely ring, I do love her and little blind
girls.

Men and boys do make carpets in mills. Wool
grows on sheep. Men do cut sheep's wool off with
large shears, and send it to the mill. Men and women
do make wool cloth in mills.

Cotton grows on large stalks in fields. Men and
boys and girls and women do pick cotton. We do make
thread and cotton dresses of cotton. Cotton has pretty
white and red flowers on it. Teacher did tear her dress.
Mildred does cry. I will nurse Nancy. Mother will buy
me lovely new aprons and dress to take to Boston. I
went to Knoxville with father and aunt. Bessie is weak
and little. Mrs. Thompson's chickens killed Leila's
chickens. Eva does sleep in my bed. I do love good
girls.

Good-by
HELEN KELLER.

The next two letters mention her visit in January to her relatives in Memphis, Tennessee. She was taken to the cotton exchange. When she felt the maps and blackboards she asked,

"Do men go to school?" She wrote on the blackboard the names of all the gentlemen present. While at Memphis she went over one of the large Mississippi steamers.

TO DR. EDWARD EVERETT HALE

Tuscumbia, Alabama, February 15th (1888).
Dear Mr. Hale,
I am happy to write you a letter this morning. Teacher told me about kind gentleman I shall be glad to read pretty story I do read stories in my book about tigers and lions and sheep.

I am coming to Boston in June to see little blind girls and I will come to see you. I went to Memphis to see grandmother and Aunt Nannie. Teacher bought me lovely new dress and cap and aprons. Little Natalie is a very weak and small baby. Father took us to see steamboat. It was on a large river. Boat is like house. Mildred is a good baby. I do love to play with little sister. Nancy was not a good child when I went to Memphis. She did cry loud. I will not write more today. I am tired.

Good-by
HELEN KELLER.

TO MR. MICHAEL ANAGNOS

Tuscumbia, Ala., Feb. 24th, 1888.
My dear Mr. Anagnos,—I'm glad to write you a letter in Braille. This morning Lucien Thompson sent me a beautiful bouquet of violets and crocuses and jonquils. Sunday Adeline Moses brought me a lovely doll. It came from New York. Her name is Adeline Keller. She can shut her eyes and bend her arms and sit down and stand up straight. She has on a pretty red dress. She is Nancy's sister and I am their mother. Allie is their

cousin. Nancy was a bad child when I went to Memphis she cried loud, I whipped her with a stick.

Mildred does feed little chickens with crumbs. I love to play with little sister.

Teacher and I went to Memphis to see aunt Nannie and grandmother. Louise is aunt Nannie's child. Teacher bought me a lovely new dress and gloves and stockings and collars and grandmother made me warm flannels, and aunt Nannie made me aprons. Lady made me a pretty cap. I went to see Robert and Mr. Graves and Mrs. Graves and little Natalie, and Mr. Farris and Mr. Mayo and Mary and everyone. I do love Robert and teacher. She does not want me to write more today. I feel tired.

I found box of candy in Mr. Grave's pocket. Father took us to see steam boat it is like house. Boat was on very large river. Yates plowed yard today to plant grass. Mule pulled plow. Mother will make garden of vegetables. Father will plant melons and peas and beans.

Cousin Bell will come to see us Saturday. Mother will make ice-cream for dinner, we will have ice-cream and cake for dinner. Lucien Thompson is sick. I am sorry for him.

Teacher and I went to walk in the yard, and I learned about how flowers and trees grow. Sun rises in the east and sets in the west. Sheffield is north and Tuscumbia is south. We will go to Boston in June. I will have fun with little blind girls.

Good bye
HELEN KELLER.

"Uncle Morrie" of the next letter is Mr. Morrison Heady, of Normandy, Kentucky, who lost his sight and hearing when he was a boy. He is the author of some commendable verses.

TO MR. MORRISON HEADY

Tuscumbia, Ala., March 1st 1888.

My dear uncle Morrie,—I am happy to write you a letter, I do love you, and I will hug and kiss you when I see you.

Mr. Anagnos is coming to see me Monday. I do love to run and hop and skip with Robert in bright warm sun. I do know little girl in Lexington Ky. her name is Katherine Hobson.

I am going to Boston in June with mother and teacher, I will have fun with little blind girls, and Mr. Hale will send me pretty story. I do read stories in my book about lions and tigers and bears.

Mildred will not go to Boston, she does cry. I love to play with little sister, she is weak and small baby. Eva is better.

Yates killed ants, ants stung Yates. Yates is digging in garden. Mr. Anagnos did see oranges, they look like golden apples.

Robert will come to see me Sunday when sun shines and I will have fun with him. My cousin Frank lives in Louisville. I will come to Memphis again to see Mr. Farris and Mrs. Graves and Mr. Mayo and Mr. Graves. Natalie is a good girl and does not cry, and she will be big and Mrs. Graves is making short dresses for her. Natalie has a little carriage. Mr. Mayo has been to Duck Hill and he brought sweet flowers home.

> With much love and a kiss
> HELEN A. KELLER.

In this account of the picnic we get an illuminating glimpse of Miss Sullivan's skill in teaching her pupil during play hours. This was a day when the child's vocabulary grew.

TO MR. MICHAEL ANAGNOS

Tuscumbia, Ala. May 3rd 1888.

Dear Mr. Anagnos.—I am glad to write to you this morning, because I love you very much. I was very happy to receive pretty book and nice candy and two letters from you. I will come to see you soon and will ask you many questions about countries and you will love good child.

Mother is making me pretty new dresses to wear in Boston and I will look lovely to see little girls and boys and you. Friday teacher and I went to a picnic with little children. We played games and ate dinner under the trees, and we found ferns and wild flowers. I walked in the woods and learned names of many trees. There are poplar and cedar and pine and oak and ash and hickory and maple trees. They make a pleasant shade and the little birds love to swing to and fro and sing sweetly up in the trees. Rabbits hop and squirrels run and ugly snakes do crawl in the woods. Geraniums and roses jasamines and japonicas are cultivated flowers. I help mother and teacher water them every night before supper.

Cousin Arthur made me a swing in the ash tree. Aunt Ev. had gone to Memphis. Uncle Frank is here. He is picking strawberries for dinner. Nancy is sick again, new teeth do make her ill. Adeline is well and she can go to Cincinnati Monday with me. Aunt Ev. will send me a boy doll, Harry will be Nancy's and Adeline's brother. Wee sister is a good girl. I am tired now and I do want to go down stairs. I send many kisses and hugs with letter.

Your darling child
HELEN KELLER

Toward the end of May Mrs. Keller, Helen, and Miss Sullivan started for Boston. On the way they spent a few days in Washington, where they saw Dr. Alexander Graham Bell and

called on President Cleveland. On May 26th they arrived in
Boston and went to the Perkins Institution; here Helen met
the little blind girls with whom she had corresponded the year
before.

Early in July she went to Brewster, Massachusetts, and
spent the rest of the summer. Here occurred her first encounter
with the sea, of which she has since written.

TO MISS MARY C. MOORE

So. Boston, Mass. Sept 1888

My dear Miss Moore
Are you very glad to receive a nice letter from your
darling little friend? I love you very dearly because
you are my friend. My precious little sister is quite
well now. She likes to sit in my little rocking-chair and
put her kitty to sleep. Would you like to see darling
little Mildred? She is a very pretty baby. Her eyes are
very big and blue, and her cheeks are soft and round
and rosy and her hair is very bright and golden. She is
very good and sweet when she does not cry loud. Next
summer Mildred will go out in the garden with me
and pick the big sweet strawberries and then she will
be very happy. I hope she will not eat too many of the
delicious fruit for they will make her very ill.

Sometimes will you please come to Alabama and
visit me? My uncle James is going to buy me a very
gentle pony and a pretty cart and I shall be very happy
to take you and Harry to ride. I hope Harry will not be
afraid of my pony. I think my father will buy me a
beautiful little brother some day. I shall be very gentle
and patient to my new little brother. When I visit many
strange countries my brother and Mildred will stay
with grandmother because they will be too small to
see a great many people and I think they would cry
loud on the great rough ocean.

When Capt. Baker gets well he will take me in his

big ship to Africa. Then I shall see lions and tigers and
monkeys. I will get a baby lion and a white monkey
and a mild bear to bring home. I had a very pleasant
time at Brewster. I went in bathing almost every day
and Carrie and Frank and little Helen and I had fun.
We splashed and jumped and waded in the deep water.
I am not afraid to float now. Can Harry float and
swim? We came to Boston last Thursday, and Mr.
Anagnos was delighted to see me, and he hugged and
kissed me. The little girls are coming back to school
next Wednesday.

Will you please tell Harry to write me a very long
letter soon? When you come to Tuscumbia to see me I
hope my father will have many sweet apples and juicy
peaches and fine pears and delicious grapes and large
water melons.

I hope you think about me and love me because I
am a good little child.

>With much love and two kisses
>From your little friend
>HELEN A. KELLER.

In this account of a visit to some friends, Helen's thought is
much what one would expect from an ordinary child of eight,
except perhaps her naïve satisfaction in the boldness of the
young gentlemen.

TO MRS. KATE ADAMS KELLER

So. Boston, Mass, Sept. 24th (1888).

My dear Mother,
I think you will be very glad to know all about my
visit to West Newton. Teacher and I had a lovely time
with many kind friends. West Newton is not far from
Boston and we went there in the steam cars very
quickly.

Mrs. Freeman and Carrie and Ethel and Frank and

Helen came to station to meet us in a huge carriage. I
was delighted to see my dear little friends and I
hugged and kissed them. Then we rode for a long time
to see all the beautiful things in West Newton. Many
very handsome houses and large soft green lawns
around them and trees and bright flowers and
fountains. The horse's name was Prince and he was
gentle and liked to trot very fast. When we went home
we saw eight rabbits and two fat puppies, and a nice
little white pony, and two wee kittens and a pretty
curly dog named Don. Pony's name was Mollie and I
had a nice ride on her back; I was not afraid, I hope
my uncle will get me a dear little pony and a little cart
very soon.

Clifton did not kiss me because he does not like to
kiss little girls. He is shy. I am very glad that Frank and
Clarence and Robbie and Eddie and Charles and
George were not very shy. I played with many little
girls and we had fun. I rode on Carrie's tricicle and
picked flowers and ate fruit and hopped and skipped
and danced and went to ride. Many ladies and
gentlemen came to see us. Lucy and Dora and Charles
were born in China. I was born in America, and Mr.
Anagnos was born in Greece. Mr. Drew says little girls
in China cannot talk on their fingers but I think when I
go to China I will teach them. Chinese nurse came to
see me, her name was Asu. She showed me a tiny atze
that very rich ladies in China wear because their feet
never grow large. Amah means a nurse. We came home
in horse cars because it was Sunday and steam cars do
not go often on Sunday. Conductors and engineers do
get very tired and go home to rest. I saw little Willie
Swan in the car and he gave me a juicy pear. He was six
years old. What did I do when I was six years old? Will
you please ask my father to come to train to meet
teacher and me? I am very sorry that Eva and Bessie
are sick. I hope I can have a nice party my birthday, and

I do want Carrie and Ethel and Frank and Helen to
come to Alabama to visit me. Will Mildred sleep with
me when I come home.

   With much love and thousand kisses.

   From your dear little daughter.

                                   HELEN A. KELLER.

Her visit to Plymouth was in July. This letter, written three
months later, shows how well she remembered her first lesson
in history.

TO MR. MORRISON HEADY

South Boston, Mass. October 1st, 1888.
My dear uncle Morrie,—I think you will be very glad
to receive a letter from your dear little friend Helen. I
am very happy to write to you because I think of you
and love you. I read pretty stories in the book you sent
me, about Charles and his boat, and Arthur and his
dream, and Rosa and the sheep.

   I have been in a large boat. It was like a ship.
Mother and teacher and Mrs. Hopkins and Mr.
Anagnos and Mr. Rodocanachi and many other friends
went to Plymouth to see many old things. I will tell
you a little story about Plymouth.

   Many years ago there lived in England many good
people, but the king and his friends were not kind and
gentle and patient with good people, because the king
did not like to have the people disobey him. People
did not like to go to church with the king; but they did
like to build very nice little churches for themselves.

   The king was very angry with the people and they
were sorry and they said, we will go away to a strange
country to live and leave very dear home and friends
and naughty king. So, they put all their things into big
boxes, and said, Good-bye. I am sorry for them
because they cried much. When they went to Holland

they did not know anyone; and they could not know what the people were talking about because they did not know Dutch. But soon they learned some Dutch words; but they loved their own language and they did not want little boys and girls to forget it and learn to talk funny Dutch. So they said, We must go to a new country far away and build schools and houses and churches and make new cities. So they put all their things in boxes and said, Good-bye to their new friends and sailed away in a large boat to find a new country. Poor people were not happy for their hearts were full of sad thoughts because they did not know much about America. I think little children must have been afraid of a great ocean for it is very strong and it makes a large boat rock and then the little children would fall down and hurt their heads. After they had been many weeks on the deep ocean where they could not see trees or flowers or grass, but just water and the beautiful sky, for ships could not sail quickly then because men did not know about engines and steam. One day a dear little baby-boy was born. His name was Peregrine White. I am very sorry that poor little Peregrine is dead now. Every day the people went upon deck to look out for land. One day there was a great shout on the ship for the people saw the land and they were full of joy because they had reached a new country safely. Little girls and boys jumped and clapped their hands. They were all glad when they stepped upon a huge rock. I did see the rock in Plymouth and a little ship like the Mayflower and the cradle that dear little Peregrine slept in and many other things that came in the Mayflower. Would you like to visit Plymouth some time and see many old things.

Now I am very tired and I will rest.

With much love and many kisses, from your little friend.

HELEN A. KELLER.

The foreign words in these two letters, the first of which was written during a visit to the kindergarten for the blind, she had been told months before, and had stowed them away in her memory. She assimilated words and practiced with them, sometimes using them intelligently, sometimes repeating them in a parrot-like fashion. Even when she did not fully understand words or ideas, she liked to set them down as though she did. It was in this way that she learned to use correctly words of sound and vision which express ideas outside of her experience. "Edith" is Edith Thomas.

TO MR. MICHAEL ANAGNOS

Roxbury, Mass. Oct. 17th, 1888.

Mon cher Monsieur Anagnos,

I am sitting by the window and the beautiful sun is shining on me. Teacher and I came to the kindergarten yesterday. There are twenty seven little children here and they are all blind. I am sorry because they cannot see much. Sometime will they have very well eyes? Poor Edith is blind and deaf and dumb. Are you very sad for Edith and me? Soon I shall go home to see my mother and my father and my dear good and sweet little sister. I hope you will come to Alabama to visit me and I will take you to ride in my little cart and I think you will like to see me on my dear little pony's back. I shall wear my lovely cap and my new riding dress. If the sun shines brightly I will take you to see Leila and Eva and Bessie. When I am thirteen years old I am going to travel in many strange and beautiful countries. I shall climb very high mountains in Norway and see much ice and snow. I hope I will not fall and hurt my head I shall visit little Lord Fauntleroy in England and he will be glad to show me his grand and very ancient castle. And we will run with the deer and feed the rabbits and catch the squirrels. I shall not be afraid of Fauntleroy's great dog Dougal. I hope Fauntleroy take me to see a very kind

queen. When I go to France I will take French. A little
French boy will say, *Parlez-vous Francais?* and I will
say, *Oui, Monsieur, vous avez un joli chapeau. Donnez
moi un baiser.* I hope you will go with me to Athens to
see the maid of Athens. She was very lovely lady and I
will talk Greek to her. I will say, *se agapo* and, *pos
echete* and I think she will say, *kalos,* and then I will say
chaere. Will you please come to see me soon and take
me to the theater? When you come I will say, *Kale
emera,* and when you go home I will say, *Kale nykta.*
Now I am too tired to write more. *Je vous time. Au
revoir*

> From your darling little friend
> HELEN A. KELLER.

TO MISS EVELINA H. KELLER

(*So. Boston, Mass. October 29, 1888.*)
My dearest Aunt,—I am coming home very soon and I
think you and every one will be very glad to see my
teacher and me. I am very happy because I have
learned much about many things. I am studying French
and German and Latin and Greek. *Se agapo* is Greek,
and it means I love thee. *J'ai une bonne petite sœur* is
French, and it means I have a good little sister. *Nous
avons un bon pere et une bonne mere* means, we have a
good father and a good mother. *Puer* is boy in Latin,
and *Mutter* is mother in German. I will teach Mildred
many languages when I come home.

> HELEN A. KELLER.

TO MRS. SOPHIA C. HOPKINS

Tuscumbia, Ala. Dec. 11th, 1888.

My dear Mrs. Hopkins:—

I have just fed my dear little pigeon. My brother
Simpson gave it to me last Sunday. I named it Annie,
for my teacher. My puppy has had his supper and gone
to bed. My rabbits are sleeping, too; and very soon I
shall go to bed. Teacher is writing letters to her friends.
Mother and father and their friends have gone to see a
huge furnace. The furnace is to make iron. The iron ore
is found in the ground; but it cannot be used until it
has been brought to the furnace and melted, and all the
dirt taken out, and just the pure iron left. Then it is all
ready to be manufactured into engines, stoves, kettles
and many other things.

Coal is found in the ground, too. Many years ago,
before people came to live on the earth, great trees and
tall grasses and huge ferns and all the beautiful flowers
covered the earth. When the leaves and the trees fell, the
water and the soil covered them; and then more trees
grew and fell also, and were buried under water and soil.
After they had all been pressed together for many
thousands of years, the wood grew very hard, like rock,
and then it was all ready for people to burn. Can you see
leaves and ferns and bark on the coal? Men go down
into the ground and dig out the coal, and steam-cars take
it to the large cities, and sell it to people to burn, to
make them warm and happy when it is cold out of
doors.

Are you very lonely and sad now? I hope you will
come to see me soon, and stay a long time.

With much love from your little friend

HELEN A. KELLER

TO MISS DELLA BENNETT

Tuscumbia, Ala., Jan 29, 1889.

My dear Miss Bennett:—I am delighted to write to you
this morning. We have just eaten our breakfast. Mildred
is running about downstairs. I have been reading in my
book about astronomers. *Astronomer* comes from the
Latin word *astra*, which means stars; and astronomers
are men who study the stars, and tell us about them.
When we are sleeping quietly in our beds, they are
watching the beautiful sky through the telescope. A
telescope is like a very strong eye. The stars are so far
away that people cannot tell much about them, without
very excellent instruments. Do you like to look out of
your window, and see little stars? Teacher says she can
see Venus from our window, and it is a large and
beautiful star. The stars are called the earth's brothers
and sisters.

There are a great many instruments besides those
which the astronomers use. A knife is an instrument to
cut with. I think the bell is an instrument, too. I will
tell you what I know about bells.

Some bells are musical and others are unmusical.
Some are very tiny and some are very large. I saw a
very large bell at Wellesley. It came from Japan. Bells
are used for many purposes. They tell us when
breakfast is ready, when to go to school, when it is
time for church, and when there is a fire. They tell
people when to go to work, and when to go home and
rest. The engine-bell tells the passengers that they
are coming to a station, and it tells the people to keep
out of the way. Sometimes very terrible accidents
happen, and many people are burned and drowned and
injured. The other day I broke my doll's head off, but
that was not a dreadful accident, because dolls do not
live and feel, like people. My little pigeons are well,
and so is my little bird. I would like to have some

clay. Teacher says it is time for me to study now.
Good-bye.

    With much love, and many kisses,

HELEN A. KELLER.

TO DR. EDWARD EVERETT HALE

Tuscumbia, Alabama, February 21st, 1889.

My dear Mr. Hale,

I am very much afraid that you are thinking in your
mind that little Helen has forgotten all about you and her
dear cousins. But I think you will be delighted to receive
this letter because then you will know that I of[ten] think
about you and I love you dearly for you are my dear
cousin. I have been at home a great many weeks now. It
made me feel very sad to leave Boston and I missed all
of my friends greatly, but of course I was glad to get
back to my lovely home once more. My darling little
sister is growing very fast. Sometimes she tries to spell
very short words on her small [fingers] but she is too
young to remember hard words. When she is older I will
teach her many things if she is patient and obedient. My
teacher says, if children learn to be patient and gentle
while they are little, that when they grow to be young
ladies and gentlemen they will not forget to be kind and
loving and brave. I hope I shall be courageous always. A
little girl in a story was not courageous. She thought she
saw little elves with tall pointed [hats] peeping from
between the bushes and dancing down the long alleys,
and the poor little girl was terrified. Did you have a
pleasant Christmas? I had many lovely presents given to
me. The other day I had a fine party. All of my dear little
friends came to see me. We played games, and ate ice-
cream and cake and fruit. Then we had great fun. The
sun is shining brightly to-day and I hope we shall go to
ride if the roads are dry. In a few days the beautiful
spring will be here. I am very glad because I love the

warm sunshine and the fragrant flowers. I think Flowers grow to make people happy and good. I have four dolls now. Cedric is my little boy, he is named for Lord Fauntleroy. He has big brown eyes and long golden hair and pretty round cheeks. Ida is my baby. A lady brought her to me from Paris. She can drink milk like a real baby. Lucy is a fine young lady. She has on a dainty lace dress and satin slippers. Poor old Nancy is growing old and very feeble. She is almost an invalid. I have two tame pigeons and a tiny canary bird. Jumbo is very strong and faithful. He will not let anything harm us at night. I go to school every day I am studying reading, writing, arithmetic, geography and language. My Mother and teacher send you and Mrs. Hale their greetings and Mildred sends you a kiss.

With much love and kisses, from your

Affectionate cousin
HELEN A. KELLER.

During the winter Miss Sullivan and her pupil were working at Helen's home in Tuscumbia, and to good purpose, for by spring Helen had learned to write idiomatic English. After May, 1889, I find almost no inaccuracies, except some evident slips of the pencil. She uses words precisely and makes easy, fluent sentences.

TO MR. MICHAEL ANAGNOS

Tuscumbia, Ala., May 18, 1889.

My Dear Mr. Anagnos:—You cannot imagine how delighted I was to receive a letter from you last evening. I am very sorry that you are going so far away. We shall miss you very, very much. I would love to visit many beautiful cities with you. When I was in Huntsville I saw Dr. Bryson, and he told me that he had been to Rome and Athens and Paris and London. He had climbed the high mountains in Switzerland and

visited beautiful churches in Italy and France, and he
saw a great many ancient castles. I hope you will
please write to me from all the cities you visit. When
you go to Holland please give my love to the lovely
princess Wilhelmina. She is a dear little girl, and when
she is old enough she will be the queen of Holland. If
you go to Roumania please ask the good queen
Elizabeth about her little invalid brother, and tell her
that I am very sorry that her darling little girl died. I
should like to send a kiss to Vittorio, the little prince of
Naples, but teacher says she is afraid you will not
remember so many messages. When I am thirteen
years old I shall visit them all myself.

I thank you very much for the beautiful story about
Lord Fauntleroy, and so does teacher.

I am so glad that Eva is coming to stay with me this
summer. We will have fine times together. Give
Howard my love, and tell him to answer my letter.
Thursday we had a picnic. It was very pleasant out in
the shady woods, and we all enjoyed the picnic very
much.

Mildred is out in the yard playing, and mother is
picking the delicious strawberries. Father and Uncle
Frank are down town. Simpson is coming home soon.
Mildred and I had our pictures taken while we were in
Huntsville. I will send you one.

The roses have been beautiful. Mother has a great
many fine roses. The La France and the Lamarque are
the most fragrant; but the Marechal Neil, Solfaterre,
Jacqueminot, Nipheots, Etoile de Lyon, Papa Gontier,
Gabrielle Drevet and the Perle des Jardines are all
lovely roses.

Please give the little boys and girls my love. I think
of them every day and I love them dearly in my heart.
When you come home from Europe I hope you will be
all well and very happy to get home again. Do not

forget to give my love to Miss Calliope Kehayia and
Mr. Francis Demetrios Kalopothakes.

> Lovingly, your little friend,
> HELEN ADAMS KELLER.

Like a good many of Helen Keller's early letters, this to her
French teacher is her re-phrasing of a story. It shows how
much the gift of writing is, in the early stages of its development, the gift of mimicry.

TO MISS FANNIE S. MARRETT

Tuscumbia, Ala., May 17, 1889.

My Dear Miss Marrett—I am thinking about a dear
little girl, who wept very hard. She wept because her
brother teased her very much. I will tell you what he
did, and I think you will feel very sorry for the little
child. She had a most beautiful doll given her. Oh, it
was a lovely and delicate doll! but the little girl's
brother, a tall lad, had taken the doll, and set it up in a
high tree in the garden, and had run away. The little
girl could not reach the doll, and could not help it
down, and therefore she cried. The doll cried, too, and
stretched out its arms from among the green
branches, and looked distressed. Soon the dismal
night would come—and was the doll to sit up in the
tree all night, and by herself? The little girl could not
endure that thought. "I will stay with you," said she to
the doll, although she was not at all courageous.
Already she began to see quite plainly the little elves
in their tall pointed hats, dancing down the dusky
alleys, and peeping from between the bushes, and they
seemed to come nearer and nearer; and she stretched
her hands up towards the tree in which the doll sat and
they laughed, and pointed their fingers at her. How
terrified was the little girl; but if one has not done
anything wrong, these strange little elves cannot harm

one. "Have I done anything wrong? Ah, yes!" said the
little girl. "I have laughed at the poor duck, with the
red rag tied round its leg. It hobbled, and that made
me laugh; but it is wrong to laugh at the poor
animals!".

Is it not a pitiful story? I hope the father punished
the naughty little boy. Shall you be very glad to see
my teacher next Thursday? She is going home to rest,
but she will come back to me next autumn.

Lovingly, your little friend,
HELEN A. KELLER.

TO MISS MARY E. RILEY

Tuscumbia, Ala., May 27, 1889.

My Dear Miss Riley:—I wish you were here in the
warm, sunny south today. Little sister and I would take
you out into the garden, and pick the delicious
raspberries and a few strawberries for you. How would
you like that? The strawberries are nearly all gone. In
the evening, when it is cool and pleasant, we would
walk in the yard, and catch the grasshoppers and
butterflies. We would talk about the birds and flowers
and grass and Jumbo and Pearl. If you liked, we would
run and jump and hop and dance, and be very happy. I
think you would enjoy hearing the mocking-birds sing.
One sits on the twig of a tree, just beneath our window,
and he fills the air with his glad songs. But I am afraid
you cannot come to Tuscumbia; so I will write to you,
and send you a sweet kiss and my love. How is Dick?
Daisy is happy, but she would be happy ever if she had
a little mate. My little children are all well except
Nancy, and she is quite feeble. My grandmother and
aunt Corinne are here. Grandmother is going to make
me two new dresses. Give my love to all the little girls,
and tell them that Helen loves them very, very much.
Eva sends love to all.

   With much love and many kisses, from your
affectionate little friend,

                               HELEN ADAMS KELLER.

During the summer, Miss Sullivan was away from Helen for
three months and a half, the first separation of teacher and
pupil. Only once afterward in fifteen years was their constant
companionship broken for more than a few days at a time.

TO MISS ANNE MANSFIELD SULLIVAN

Tuscumbia, Ala., August 7, 1889.
Dearest Teacher—I am very glad to write to you this
evening, for I have been thinking much about you all
day. I am sitting on the piazza, and my little white
pigeon is perched on the back of my chair, watching me
write. Her little brown mate has flown away with the
other birds; but Annie is not sad, for she likes to stay
with me. Fauntleroy is asleep upstairs, and Nancy is
putting Lucy to bed. Perhaps the mocking bird is singing
them to sleep. All the beautiful flowers are in bloom
now. The air is sweet with the perfume of jasmines,
heliotropes and roses. It is getting warm here now, so
father is going to take us to the Quarry on the 20th of
August. I think we shall have a beautiful time out in the
cool, pleasant woods. I will write and tell you all the
pleasant things we do. I am so glad that Lester and
Henry are good little infants. Give them many sweet
kisses for me.
   What was the name of the little boy who fell in love
with the beautiful star? Eva has been telling me a story
about a lovely little girl named Heidi. Will you please
send it to me? I shall be delighted to have a typewriter.
   Little Arthur is growing very fast. He has on short
dresses now. Cousin Leila thinks he will walk in a little
while. Then I will take his soft chubby hand in mine,
and go out in the bright sunshine with him. He will

pull the largest roses, and chase the gayest butterflies. I
will take very good care of him, and not let him fall
and hurt himself. Father and some other gentlemen
went hunting yesterday. Father killed thirty-eight birds.
We had some of them for supper, and they were very
nice. Last Monday Simpson shot a pretty crane. The
crane is a large and strong bird. His wings are as long
as my arm, and his bill is as long as my foot. He eats
little fishes, and other small animals. Father says he
can fly nearly all day without stopping.

Mildred is the dearest and sweetest little maiden in
the world. She is very roguish, too. Sometimes, when
mother does not know it, she goes out into the
vineyard, and gets her apron full of delicious grapes. I
think she would like to put her two soft arms around
your neck and hug you.

Sunday I went to church. I love to go to church,
because I like to see my friends.

A gentleman gave me a beautiful card. It was a
picture of a mill, near a beautiful brook. There was a
boat floating on the water, and the fragrant lilies were
growing all around the boat. Not far from the mill
there was an old house, with many trees growing close
to it. There were eight pigeons on the roof of the
house, and a great dog on the step. Pearl is a very
proud mother-dog now. She has eight puppies, and she
thinks there never were such fine puppies as hers.

I read in my books every day. I love them very, very,
very much. I do want you to come back to me soon. I
miss you so very, very much. I cannot know about
many things, when my dear teacher is not here. I send
you five thousand kisses, and more love than I can tell.
I send Mrs. H. much love and a kiss.

From your affectionate little pupil,
HELEN A. KELLER.

In the fall Helen and Miss Sullivan returned to Perkins Institution at South Boston.

TO MISS MILDRED KELLER

South Boston, Oct. 24, 1889.

My Precious Little Sister:—Good Morning. I am
going to send you a birthday gift with this letter. I hope
it will please you very much, because it makes me
happy to send it. The dress is blue like your eyes, and
candy is sweet just like your dear little self. I think
mother will be glad to make the dress for you, and
when you wear it you will look as pretty as a rose. The
picture-book will tell you all about many strange and
wild animals. You must not be afraid of them. They
cannot come out of the picture to harm you.

I go to school every day, and I learn many new
things. At eight I study arithmetic. I like that. At nine I
go to the gymnasium with the little girls and we have
great fun. I wish you could be here to play three little
squirrels, and two gentle doves, and to make a pretty
nest for a dear little robin. The mocking bird does not
live in the cold north. At ten I study about the earth on
which we all live. At eleven I talk with teacher and at
twelve I study zoölogy. I do not know what I shall do
in the afternoon yet.

Now, my darling little Mildred, good bye. Give
father and mother a great deal of love and many hugs
and kisses for me. Teacher sends her love too.

From your loving sister,
HELEN A. KELLER.

TO MR. WILLIAM WADE

South Boston, Mass., Nov. 20, 1889.

My Dear Mr. Wade:—I have just received a letter from
my mother, telling me that the beautiful mastiff puppy
you sent me had arrived in Tuscumbia safely. Thank
you very much for the nice gift. I am very sorry that I
was not at home to welcome her; but my mother and

my baby sister will be very kind to her while her mistress is away. I hope she is not lonely and unhappy. I think puppies can feel very home-sick, as well as little girls. I should like to call her Lioness, for your dog. May I? I hope she will be very faithful,—and brave, too.

I am studying in Boston, with my dear teacher. I learn a great many new and wonderful things. I study about the earth, and the animals, and I like arithmetic exceedingly. I learn many new words, too. *Exceedingly* is one that I learned yesterday. When I see Lioness I will tell her many things which will surprise her greatly. I think she will laugh when I tell her she is a vertebrate, a mammal, a quadruped; and I shall be very sorry to tell her that she belongs to the order Carnivora. I study French, too. When I talk French to Lioness I will call her *mon beau chien.* Please tell Lion that I will take good care of Lioness. I shall be happy to have a letter from you when you like to write to me.

From your loving little friend,
HELEN A. KELLER.

P.S. I am studying at the Institution for the blind.
H. A. K.

This letter is endorsed in Whittier's hand, "Helen A. Keller— deaf dumb and blind—aged nine years." "Browns" is a lapse of the pencil for "brown eyes."

TO JOHN GREENLEAF WHITTIER

Inst. for the Blind, So. Boston, Mass., Nov. 27, 1889.
Dear Poet,
I think you will be surprised to receive a letter from a little girl whom you do not know, but I thought you would be glad to hear that your beautiful poems make me very happy. Yesterday I read "In School Days" and

"My Playmate," and I enjoyed them greatly. I was very sorry that the poor little girl with the browns and the "tangled golden curls" died. It is very pleasant to live here in our beautiful world. I cannot see the lovely things with my eyes, but my mind can see them all, and so I am joyful all the day long.

When I walk out in my garden I cannot see the beautiful flowers but I know that they are all around me; for is not the air sweet with their fragrance? I know too that the tiny lily-bells are whispering pretty secrets to their companions else they would not look so happy. I love you very dearly, because you have taught me so many things about flowers, and birds, and people. Now I must say, good-bye. I hope [you] will enjoy the Thanksgiving very much.

From your loving little friend,
HELEN A. KELLER.

Whittier's reply, to which there is a reference in the following letter, has been lost.

TO MRS. KATE ADAMS KELLER

South Boston, Mass., Dec. 3, 1889.

My Dear Mother:—Your little daughter is very happy to write to you this beautiful morning. It is cold and rainy here to-day. Yesterday the Countess of Meath came again to see me. She gave me a beautiful bunch of violets. Her little girls are named Violet and May. The Earl said he should be delighted to visit Tuscumbia the next time he comes to America. Lady Meath said she would like to see your flowers, and hear the mockingbirds sing. When I visit England they want me to come to see them, and stay a few weeks. They will take me to see the Queen.

I had a lovely letter from the poet Whittier. He loves me. Mr. Wade wants teacher and me to come and see

him next spring. May we go? He said you must feed
Lioness from your hand, because she will be more
gentle if she does not eat with other dogs.

Mr. Wilson came to call on us one Thursday. I was
delighted to receive the flowers from home. They came
while we were eating breakfast, and my friends
enjoyed them with me. We had a very nice dinner on
Thanksgiving day—turkey and plum-pudding. Last
week I visited a beautiful art store. I saw a great many
statues, and the gentleman gave me an angel.

Sunday I went to church on board a great warship.
After the services were over the soldier-sailors showed
us around. There were four hundred and sixty sailors.
They were very kind to me. One carried me in his arms
so that my feet would not touch the water. They wore
blue uniforms and queer little caps. There was a
terrible fire Thursday. Many stores were burned, and
four men were killed. I am very sorry for them. Tell
father, please, to write to me. How is dear little sister?
Give her many kisses for me. Now I must close. With
much love, from your darling child,

HELEN A. KELLER.

TO MRS. KATE ADAMS KELLER

So. Boston, Mass., Dec. 24, 1889.

My dear Mother,
Yesterday I sent you a little Christmas box. I am very
sorry that I could not send it before so that you would
receive it to morrow, but I could not finish the watch-
case any sooner. I made all of the gifts myself, excepting
father's handkerchief. I wish I could have made father a
gift too, but I did not have sufficient time. I hope you
will like your watch-case, for it made me very happy to
make it for you. You must keep your lovely new montre
in it. If it is too warm in Tuscumbia for little sister to
wear her pretty mittens she can keep them because her

sister made them for her. I imagine she will have fun
with the little toy man. Tell her to shake him, and then he
will blow his trumpet. I thank my dear kind father for
sending me some money, to buy gifts for my friends. I
love to make everybody happy. I should like to be at
home on Christmas day. We would be very happy
together. I think of my beautiful home every day. Please
do not forget to send me some pretty presents to hang on
my tree. I am going to have a Christmas tree, in the
parlor and teacher will hang all of my gifts upon it. It
will be a funny tree. All of the girls have gone home to
spend Christmas. Teacher and I are the only babies left
for Mrs. Hopkins to care for. Teacher has been sick in
bed for many days. Her throat was very sore and the
doctor thought she would have to go away to the
hospital. But she is better now. I have not been sick at
all. The little girls are well too. Friday I am going to
spend the day with my little friends Carrie, Ethel, Frank
and Helen Freeman. We will have great fun I am sure.

Mr. and Miss Endicott came to see me, and I went to
ride in the carriage. They are going to give me a lovely
present, but I cannot guess what it will be. Sammy has a
dear new brother. He is very soft and delicate yet. Mr.
Anagnos is in Athens now. He is delighted because I am
here. Now I must say, goodbye. I hope I have written my
letter nicely, but it is very difficult to write on this paper
and teacher is not here to give me better. Give many
kisses to little sister and much love to all. Lovingly.

                                                    HELEN.

TO DR. EDWARD EVERETT HALE

South Boston, Jan. 8, 1890.

My dear Mr. Hale:
The beautiful shells came last night. I thank you very
much for them. I shall always keep them, and it will

make me very happy to think that you found them, on
that far away island, from which Columbus sailed to
discover our dear country. When I am eleven years old
it will be four hundred years since he started with the
three small ships to cross the great strange ocean. He
was very brave. The little girls were delighted to see
the lovely shells. I told them all I knew about them.
Are you very glad you could make so many happy? I
am. I should be very happy to come and teach you the
Braille sometime, if you have time to learn, but I am
afraid you are too busy. A few days ago I received a
little box of English violets from Lady Meath. The
flowers were wilted, but the kind thought which came
with them was as sweet and as fresh as newly pulled
violets.

    With loving greeting to the little cousins, and Mrs.
Hale and a sweet kiss for yourself,

From your little friend,
HELEN A. KELLER.

This, the first of Helen's letters to Dr. Holmes, written soon after a visit to him, he published in "Over the Teacups."

TO DR. OLIVER WENDELL HOLMES

    South Boston, Mass., March 1, 1890.
Dear, Kind Poet:—I have thought of you many times
since that bright Sunday when I bade you goodbye;
and I am going to write you a letter, because I love
you. I am sorry that you have no little children to play
with you sometimes; but I think you are very happy
with your books, and your many, many friends. On
Washington's birthday a great many people came here
to see the blind children; and I read for them from
your poems, and showed them some beautiful shells,
which came from a little island near Palos.

I am reading a very sad story, called "Little Jakey." Jakey was the sweetest little fellow you can imagine, but he was poor and blind. I used to think—when I was small, and before I could read—that everybody was always happy, and at first it made me very sad to know about pain and great sorrow; but now I know that we could never learn to be brave and patient, if there were only joy in the world.

I am studying about insects in zoölogy, and I have learned many things about butterflies. They do not make honey for us, like the bees, but many of them are as beautiful as the flowers they light upon, and they always delight the hearts of little children. They live a gay life, flitting from flower to flower, sipping the drops of honeydew, without a thought for the morrow. They are just like little boys and girls when they forget books and studies, and run away to the woods and the fields, to gather wild flowers, or wade in the ponds for fragrant lilies, happy in the bright sunshine.

If my little sister comes to Boston next June, will you let me bring her to see you? She is a lovely baby, and I am sure you will love her.

Now I must tell my gentle poet good-bye, for I have a letter to write home before I go to bed.

From your loving little friend,
HELEN A. KELLER.

TO MISS SARAH FULLER*

South Boston, Mass., April 3, 1890.

My dear Miss Fuller,

My heart is full of joy this beautiful morning, because I have learned to speak many new words, and I can make a few sentences. Last evening I went out in the yard and spoke to the moon. I said, "O! moon come to me!" Do

you think the lovely moon was glad that I could speak to
her? How glad my mother will be. I can hardly wait for
June to come I am so eager to speak to her and to my
precious little sister. Mildred could not understand me
when I spelled with my fingers, but now she will sit in
my lap and I will tell her many things to please her, and
we shall be so happy together. Are you very, very happy
because you can make so many people happy? I think
you are very kind and patient, and I love you very
dearly. My teacher told me Tuesday that you wanted to
know how I came to wish to talk with my mouth. I will
tell you all about it, for I remember my thoughts
perfectly. When I was a very little child I used to sit in
my mother's lap all the time, because I was very timid,
and did not like to be left by myself. And I would keep
my little hand on her face all the while, because it
amused me to feel her face and lips move when she
talked with people. I did not know then what she was
doing, for I was quite ignorant of all things. Then when I
was older I learned to play with my nurse and the little
negro children and I noticed that they kept moving their
lips just like my mother, so I moved mine too, but
sometimes it made me angry and I would hold my
playmates' mouths very hard. I did not know then that it
was very naughty to do so. After a long time my dear
teacher came to me, and taught me to communicate with
my fingers and I was satisfied and happy. But when I
came to school in Boston I met some deaf people who
talked with their mouths like all other people, and one
day a lady who had been to Norway came to see me, and
told me of a blind and deaf girl† she had seen in that far
away land who had been taught to speak and understand
others when they spoke to her. This good and happy
news delighted me exceedingly, for then I was sure that I
should learn also. I tried to make sounds like my little
playmates, but teacher told me that the voice was very

delicate and sensitive and that it would injure it to make incorrect sounds, and promised to take me to see a kind and wise lady who would teach me rightly. That lady was yourself. Now I am as happy as the little birds, because I can speak and perhaps I shall sing too. All of my friends will be so surprised and glad.

Your loving little pupil,
HELEN A. KELLER.

* Miss Fuller gave Helen Keller her first lesson in articulation. For an account of this see Part III, Chapter IV.

† Ragnhild Kaata

When the Perkins Institution closed for the summer, Helen and Miss Sullivan went to Tuscumbia. This was the first home-going after she had learned to "talk with her mouth."

TO REV. PHILLIPS BROOKS

Tuscumbia, Alabama, July 14, 1890.

My dear Mr. Brooks, I am very glad to write to you this beautiful day because you are my kind friend and I love you, and because I wish to know many things. I have been at home three weeks, and Oh, how happy I have been with dear mother and father and precious little sister. I was very, very sad to part with all of my friends in Boston, but I was so eager to see my baby sister I could hardly wait for the train to take me home. But I tried very hard to be patient for teacher's sake. Mildred has grown much taller and stronger than she was when I went to Boston, and she is the sweetest and dearest little child in the world. My parents were delighted to hear me speak, and I was overjoyed to give them such a happy surprise. I think it is so pleasant to make everybody happy. Why does the dear Father in heaven think it best for us to have very great sorrow

sometimes? I am always happy and so was Little Lord
Fauntleroy, but dear Little Jakey's life was full of
sadness. God did not put the light in Jakey's eyes and
he was blind, and his father was not gentle and loving.
Do you think poor Jakey loved his Father in heaven
more because his other father was unkind to him? How
did God tell people that his home was in heaven?
When people do very wrong and hurt animals and treat
children unkindly God is grieved, but what will he do
to them to teach them to be pitiful and loving? I think
he will tell them how dearly He loves them and that He
wants them to be good and happy, and they will not
wish to grieve their father who loves them so much,
and they will want to please him in everything they do,
so they will love each other and do good to everyone,
and be kind to animals.

Please tell me something that you know about God.
It makes me happy to know much about my loving
Father, who is good and wise. I hope you will write to
your little friend when you have time. I should like
very much to see you to-day Is the sun very hot in
Boston now? this afternoon if it is cool enough I shall
take Mildred for a ride on my donkey. Mr. Wade sent
Neddy to me, and he is the prettiest donkey you can
imagine. My great dog Lioness goes with us when we
ride to protect us. Simpson, that is my brother, brought
me some beautiful pond lilies yesterday—he is a very
brother to me.

Teacher sends you her kind remembrances, and
father and mother also send their regards.

> From your loving little friend,
> HELEN A. KELLER.

DR. BROOKS'S REPLY

London, August 3, 1890.

My Dear Helen—I was very glad indeed to get your letter. It has followed me across the ocean and found me in this magnificent great city which I should like to tell you all about if I could take time for it and make my letter long enough. Some time when you come and see me in my study in Boston I shall be glad to talk to you about it all if you care to hear.

But now I want to tell you how glad I am that you are so happy and enjoying your home so very much. I can almost think I see you with your father and mother and little sister, with all the brightness of the beautiful country about you, and it makes me very glad to know how glad you are.

I am glad also to know, from the questions which you ask me, what you are thinking about. I do not see how we can help thinking about God when He is so good to us all the time. Let me tell you how it seems to me that we come to know about our heavenly Father. It is from the power of love which is in our own hearts. Love is at the soul of everything. Whatever has not the power of loving must have a very dreary life indeed. We like to think that the sunshine and the winds and the trees are able to love in some way of their own, for it would make us know that they were happy if we know that they could love. And so God who is the greatest and happiest of all beings is the most loving too. All the love that is in our hearts comes from him, as all the light which is in the flowers comes from the sun. And the more we love the more near we are to God and His Love.

I told you that I was very happy because of your happiness. Indeed I am. So are your Father and your Mother and your Teacher and all your friends. But do you not think that God is happy too because you are happy? I am sure He is. And He is happier than any of

us because He is greater than any of us, and also
because He not merely *sees* your happiness as we do,
but He also *made* it. He gives it to you as the sun gives
light and color to the rose. And we are always most
glad of what we not merely see our friends enjoy, but
of what we give them to enjoy. Are we not?

But God does not only want us to be *happy;* He
wants us to be *good.* He wants that most of all. He
knows that we can be really happy only when we are
good. A great deal of the trouble that is in the world is
medicine which is very bad to take, but which it is
good to take because it makes us better. We see how
good people may be in great trouble when we think of
Jesus who was the greatest sufferer that ever lived and
yet was the best Being and so, I am sure, the happiest
Being that the world has ever seen.

I love to tell you about God. But He will tell you
Himself by the love which He will put into your heart
if you ask Him. And Jesus, who is His Son, but is
nearer to Him than all of us His other Children, came
into the world on purpose to tell us all about our
Father's Love. If you read His words, you will see how
full His heart is of the love of God. "We *know* that He
loves us," He says. He loved men Himself and though
they were very cruel to Him and at last killed Him, He
was willing to die for them because He loved them so.
And, Helen, He loves men still, and He loves us, and
He tells us that we may love Him.

And so love is everything. And if anybody asks you,
or if you ask yourself what God is, answer, "God is
Love." That is the beautiful answer which the Bible
gives.

All this is what you are to think of and to
understand more and more as you grow older. Think
of it now, and let it make every blessing brighter
because your dear Father sends it to you.

You will come back to Boston I hope soon after I
do. I shall be there by the middle of September. I shall

want you to tell me all about everything, and not forget the Donkey.

I send my kind remembrance to your father and mother, and to your teacher. I wish I could see your little sister.

Good Bye, dear Helen. Do write to me soon again, directing your letter to Boston.

Your affectionate friend
PHILLIPS BROOKS.

DR. HOLMES'S REPLY
To a letter which has been lost.

Beverly Farms, Mass., August 1, 1890.

My Dear Little Friend Helen:

I received your welcome letter several days ago, but I have so much writing to do that I am apt to make my letters wait a good while before they get answered.

It gratifies me very much to find that you remember me so kindly. Your letter is charming, and I am greatly pleased with it. I rejoice to know that you are well and happy. I am very much delighted to hear of your new acquisition that you "talk with your mouth" as well as with your fingers. What a curious thing *speech* is! The tongue is so serviceable a member (taking all sorts of shapes, just as is wanted),—the teeth, the lips, the roof of the mouth; all ready to help, and so heap up the sound of the voice into the solid bits which we call consonants, and make room for the curiously shaped breathings which we call vowels! You have studied all this, I don't doubt, since you have practised vocal speaking.

I am surprised at the mastery of language which your letter shows. It almost makes me think the world would get along as well without seeing and hearing as with them. Perhaps people would be better in a great many ways, for they could not fight as they do now. Just think of an army of blind people, with guns and cannon! Think of the poor drummers! Of what use would they and their drumsticks be? You are spared the pain of many sights and sounds, which you are only too happy in escaping. Then think how much kindness you are sure of as long as you live. Everybody will feel an interest in dear little Helen; everybody will want to do something for her; and, if she becomes an ancient, gray-haired woman, she is still sure of being thoughtfully cared for.

Your parents and friends must take great satisfaction in your progress. It does great credit, not only to you, but to your instructors, who have so broken down the walls that seemed to shut you in that now your outlook seems more bright and cheerful than that of many seeing and hearing children.

Good-bye, dear little Helen! With every kind wish from your friend,

OLIVER WENDELL HOLMES.

This letter was written to some gentlemen in Gardiner, Maine, who named a lumber vessel after her.

TO MESSRS. BRADSTREET

Tuscumbia, Ala., July 14, 1890.

My Dear, Kind Friends:—I thank you very, very much for naming your beautiful new ship for me. It makes me very happy to know that I have kind and loving friends in the far-away State of Maine. I did not imagine, when I studied about the forests of Maine, that a strong and beautiful ship would go sailing all over the world, carrying wood from those rich forests, to build pleasant homes and schools and churches in distant countries. I hope the great ocean will love the new Helen, and let her sail over its blue waves

peacefully. Please tell the brave sailors, who have
charge of the HELEN KELLER, that little Helen who
stays at home will often think of them with loving
thoughts. I hope I shall see you and my beautiful
namesake some time.

    With much love, from your little friend,

HELEN A. KELLER.

Helen and Miss Sullivan returned to the Perkins Institution
early in November.

TO MRS. KATE ADAMS KELLER

South Boston, Nov. 10, 1890.

My Dearest Mother:—My heart has been full of
thoughts of you and my beautiful home ever since we
parted so sadly on Wednesday night. How I wish I
could see you this lovely morning, and tell you all that
has happened since I left home! And my darling little
sister, how I wish I could give her a hundred kisses!
And my dear father, how he would like to hear about
our journey! But I cannot see you and talk to you, so I
will write and tell you all that I can think of.

    We did not reach Boston until Saturday morning. I
am sorry to say that our train was delayed in several
places, which made us late in reaching New York.
When we got to Jersey City at six o'clock Friday
evening we were obliged to cross the Harlem River in
a ferry-boat. We found the boat and the transfer
carriage with much less difficulty than teacher
expected. When we arrived at the station they told us
that the train did not leave for Boston until eleven
o'clock, but that we could take the sleeper at nine,
which we did. We went to bed and slept until morning.
When we awoke we were in Boston. I was delighted to
get there, though I was much disappointed because we
did not arrive on Mr. Anagnos' birthday. We surprised

our dear friends, however, for they did not expect us
Saturday; but when the bell rung Miss Marrett
guessed who was at the door, and Mrs. Hopkins
jumped up from the breakfast table and ran to the door
to meet us; she was indeed much astonished to see us.
After we had some breakfast we went up to see Mr.
Anagnos. I was overjoyed to see my dearest and
kindest friend once more. He gave me a beautiful
watch. I have it pinned to my dress. I tell everybody
the time when they ask me. I have only seen Mr.
Anagnos twice. I have many questions to ask him
about the countries he has been travelling in. But I
suppose he is very busy now.

The hills in Virginia were very lovely. Jack Frost
had dressed them in gold and crimson. The view was
most charmingly picturesque. Pennsylvania is a very
beautiful State. The grass was as green as though it
was springtime, and the golden ears of corn gathered
together in heaps in the great fields looked very pretty.
In Harrisburg we saw a donkey like Neddy. How I
wish I could see my own donkey and my dear
Lioness! Do they miss their mistress very much? Tell
Mildred she must be kind to them for my sake.

Our room is pleasant and comfortable.

My typewriter was much injured coming. The case
was broken and the keys are nearly all out. Teacher is
going to see if it can be fixed.

There are many new books in the library. What a
nice time I shall have reading them! I have already
read Sara Crewe. It is a very pretty story, and I will
tell it to you some time. Now, sweet mother, your little
girl must say good-bye.

With much love to father, Mildred, you and all the
dear friends, lovingly your little daughter,

                              HELEN A. KELLER.

TO JOHN GREENLEAF WHITTIER

South Boston, Dec. 17, 1890.

Dear Kind Poet,

This is your birthday; that was the first thought which
came into my mind when I awoke this morning; and
it made me glad to think I could write you a letter
and tell you how much your little friends love their
sweet poet and his birthday. This evening they are
going to entertain their friends with readings from
your poems and music. I hope the swift winged
messengers of love will be here to carry some of the
sweet melody to you, in your little study by the
Merrimac. At first I was very sorry when I found that
the sun had hidden his shining face behind dull
clouds, but afterwards I thought why he did it, and
then I was happy. The sun knows that you like to see
the world covered with beautiful white snow and so he
kept back all his brightness, and let the little crystals
form in the sky. When they are ready, they will softly
fall and tenderly cover every object. Then the sun will
appear in all his radiance and fill the world with light.
If I were with you to-day I would give you eighty-
three kisses, one for each year you have lived.
Eighty-three years seems very long to me. Does it
seem long to you? I wonder how many years there will
be in eternity. I am afraid I cannot think about so
much time. I received the letter which you wrote to
me last summer, and I thank you for it. I am staying in
Boston now at the Institution for the Blind, but I have
not commenced my studies yet, because my dearest
friend, Mr. Anagnos wants me to rest and play a great
deal.

Teacher is well and sends her kind remembrance to
you. The happy Christmas time is almost here! I can
hardly wait for the fun to begin! I hope your
Christmas Day will be a very happy one and that the

New Year will be full of brightness and joy for you
and every one.

From your little friend
HELEN A. KELLER.

WHITTIER'S REPLY

My Dear Young Friend—I was very glad to have such
a pleasant letter on my birthday. I had two or three
hundred others and thine was one of the most welcome
of all. I must tell thee about how the day passed at Oak
Knoll. Of course the sun did not shine, but we had
great open wood fires in the rooms, which were all
very sweet with roses and other flowers, which were
sent to me from distant friends; and fruits of all kinds
from California and other places. Some relatives and
dear old friends were with me through the day. I do not
wonder thee thinks eighty-three years a long time, but
to me it seems but a very little while since I was a boy
no older than thee, playing on the old farm at
Haverhill. I thank thee for all thy good wishes, and
wish thee as many. I am glad thee is at the Institution;
it is an excellent place. Give my best regards to Miss
Sullivan, and with a great deal of love I am

Thy old friend,
JOHN G. WHITTIER.

Tommy Stringer, who appears in several of the following letters, became blind and deaf when he was four years old. His
mother was dead and his father was too poor to take care of
him. For a while he was kept in the general hospital at
Allegheny. From here he was to be sent to an almshouse, for at
that time there was no other place for him in Pennsylvania.
Helen heard of him through Mr. J. G. Brown of Pittsburgh,
who wrote her that he had failed to secure a tutor for Tommy.
She wanted him brought to Boston, and when she was told

that money would be needed to get him a teacher, she answered, "We will raise it." She began to solicit contributions from her friends, and saved her pennies.

Dr. Alexander Graham Bell advised Tommy's friends to send him to Boston, and the trustees of the Perkins Institution agreed to admit him to the kindergarten for the blind.

Meanwhile opportunity came to Helen to make a considerable contribution to Tommy's education. The winter before, her dog Lioness had been killed, and friends set to work to raise money to buy Helen another dog. Helen asked that the contributions, which people were sending from all over America and England, be devoted to Tommy's education. Turned to this new use, the fund grew fast, and Tommy was provided for. He was admitted to the kindergarten on the sixth of April.

Miss Keller wrote lately, "I shall never forget the pennies sent by many a poor child who could ill spare them, 'for little Tommy,' or the swift sympathy with which people from far and near, whom I had never seen, responded to the dumb cry of a little captive soul for aid."

TO MR. GEORGE R. KREHL

Institution for the Blind,
South Boston, Mass., March 20, 1891.

My Dear Friend, Mr. Krehl:—I have just heard, through Mr. Wade, of your kind offer to buy me a gentle dog, and I want to thank you for the kind thought. It makes me very happy indeed to know that I have such dear friends in other lands. It makes me think that all people are good and loving. I have read that the English and Americans are cousins; but I am sure it would be much truer to say that we are brothers and sisters. My friends have told me about your great and magnificent city, and I have read a great deal that wise Englishmen have written. I have begun to read "Enoch Arden," and I know several of the great poet's poems by heart. I am

eager to cross the ocean, for I want to see my English
friends and their good and wise queen. Once the Earl of
Meath came to see me, and he told me that the queen
was much beloved by her people, because of her
gentleness and wisdom. Some day you will be surprised
to see a little strange girl coming into your office; but
when you know it is the little girl who loves dogs and
all other animals, you will laugh, and I hope you will
give her a kiss, just as Mr. Wade does. He has another
dog for me, and he thinks she will be as brave and
faithful as my beautiful Lioness. And now I want to tell
you what the dog lovers in America are going to do.
They are going to send me some money for a poor little
deaf and dumb and blind child. His name is Tommy,
and he is five years old. His parents are too poor to pay
to have the little fellow sent to school; so, instead of
giving me a dog, the gentlemen are going to help make
Tommy's life as bright and joyous as mine. Is it not a
beautiful plan? Education will bring light and music
into Tommy's soul, and then he cannot help being
happy.

> From your loving little friend,
> HELEN A. KELLER.

TO DR. OLIVER WENDELL HOLMES

(South Boston, Mass., April, 1891.)

Dear Dr. Holmes:—Your beautiful words about spring
have been making music in my heart, these bright
April days. I love every word of "Spring" and "Spring
Has Come." I think you will be glad to hear that these
poems have taught me to enjoy and love the beautiful
springtime, even though I cannot see the fair, frail
blossoms which proclaim its approach, or hear the
joyous warbling of the home-coming birds. But when
I read "Spring Has Come," lo! I am not blind any

longer, for I see with your eyes and hear with your ears. Sweet Mother Nature can have no secrets from me when my poet is near. I have chosen this paper because I want the spray of violets in the corner to tell you of my grateful love. I want you to see baby Tom, the blind and deaf and dumb child who has just come to our pretty garden. He is poor and helpless and lonely now, but before another April education will have brought light and gladness into Tommy's life. If you do come, you will want to ask the kind people of Boston to help brighten Tommy's whole life. Your loving friend,

HELEN A. KELLER.

TO SIR JOHN EVERETT MILLAIS

Perkins Institution for the Blind, South Boston, Mass.,
April 30, 1891.

My Dear Mr. Millais:—Your little American sister is going to write you a letter, because she wants you to know how pleased she was to hear you were interested in our poor little Tommy, and had sent some money to help educate him. It is very beautiful to think that people far away in England feel sorry for a little helpless child in America. I used to think, when I read in my books about your great city, that when I visited it the people would be strangers to me, but now I feel differently. It seems to me that all people who have loving, pitying hearts, are not strangers to each other. I can hardly wait patiently for the time to come when I shall see my dear English friends, and their beautiful island home. My favourite poet has written some lines about England which I love very much. I think you will like them too, so I will try to write them for you.

"Hugged in the clinging billow's clasp,
  From seaweed fringe to mountain heather,
The British oak with rooted grasp
  Her slender handful holds together,
With cliffs of white and bowers of green,
  And ocean narrowing to caress her,
And hills and threaded streams between,
  Our little mother isle, God bless her!"

You will be glad to hear that Tommy has a kind lady to
teach him, and that he is a pretty, active little fellow.
He loves to climb much better than to spell, but that is
because he does not know yet what a wonderful thing
language is. He cannot imagine how very, very happy
he will be when he can tell us his thoughts, and we
can tell him how we have loved him so long.

   Tomorrow April will hide her tears and blushes
beneath the flowers of lovely May. I wonder if the
May-days in England are as beautiful as they are here.

   Now I must say good-bye. Please think of me
always as your loving little sister,

                                        HELEN A. KELLER.

TO REV. PHILLIPS BROOKS

                          So. Boston, May 1, 1891.

My Dear Mr. Brooks:
Helen sends you a loving greeting this bright May-
day. My teacher has just told me that you have been
made a bishop, and that your friends everywhere are
rejoicing because one whom they love has been
greatly honored. I do not understand very well what a
bishop's work is, but I am sure it must be good and
helpful, and I am glad that my dear friend is brave,
and wise, and loving enough to do it. It is very

beautiful to think that you can tell so many people of
the heavenly Father's tender love for all His children
even when they are not gentle and noble as He wishes
them to be. I hope the glad news which you will tell
them will make their hearts beat fast with joy and
love. I hope too, that Bishop Brooks' whole life will
be as rich in happiness as the month of May is full of
blossoms and singing birds.

> From your loving little friend,
> HELEN A. KELLER.

Before a teacher was found for Tommy and while he was
still in the care of Helen and Miss Sullivan, a reception was
held for him at the kindergarten. At Helen's request Bishop
Brooks made an address. Helen wrote letters to the newspapers which brought many generous replies. All of these she
answered herself, and she made public acknowledgment in
letters to the newspapers. This letter is to the editor of the
Boston Herald, enclosing a complete list of the subscribers.
The contributions amounted to more than sixteen hundred
dollars.

TO MR. JOHN H. HOLMES

> *South Boston, May 13, 1891.*

Editor of the *Boston Herald:*
My Dear Mr. Holmes:—Will you kindly print in the
Herald, the enclosed list? I think the readers of your
paper will be glad to know that so much has been
done for dear little Tommy, and that they will all wish
to share in the pleasure of helping him. He is very
happy indeed at the kindergarten, and is learning
something every day. He has found out that doors have
locks, and that little sticks and bits of paper can be
got into the keyhole quite easily; but he does not seem
very eager to get them out after they are in. He loves
to climb the bed-posts and unscrew the steam valves

much better than to spell, but that is because he
does not understand that words would help him to
make new and interesting discoveries. I hope that
good people will continue to work for Tommy until
his fund is completed, and education has brought
light and music into his little life. From your little
friend,

                              HELEN A. KELLER.

TO DR. OLIVER WENDELL HOLMES

South Boston, May 27, 1891.

Dear, Gentle Poet:—I fear that you will think Helen
a very troublesome little girl if she writes to you too
often; but how is she to help sending you loving and
grateful messages, when you do so much to make her
glad? I cannot begin to tell you how delighted I was
when Mr. Anagnos told me that you had sent him
some money to help educate "Baby Tom." Then I
knew that you had not forgotten the dear little child,
for the gift brought with it the thought of tender
sympathy. I am very sorry to say that Tommy has not
learned any words yet. He is the same restless little
creature he was when you saw him. But it is
pleasant to think that he is happy and playful in his
bright new home, and by and by that strange,
wonderful thing teacher calls *mind*, will begin to
spread its beautiful wings and fly away in search of
knowledge-land. Words are the mind's wings, are
they not?

I have been to Andover since I saw you, and I was
greatly interested in all that my friends told me about
Phillips Academy, because I knew you had been
there, and I felt it was a place dear to you. I tried to
imagine my gentle poet when he was a school-boy,
and I wondered if it was in Andover he learned the

songs of the birds and the secrets of the shy little woodland children. I am sure his heart was always full of music, and in God's beautiful world he must have heard love's sweet replying. When I came home teacher read to me "The School-boy," for it is not in our print.

Did you know that the blind children are going to have their commencement exercises in Tremont Temple, next Tuesday afternoon? I enclose a ticket, hoping that you will come. We shall all be proud and happy to welcome our poet friend. I shall recite about the beautiful cities of sunny Italy. I hope our kind friend Dr. Ellis will come too, and take Tom in his arms.

　　With much love and a kiss, from your little friend,
　　　　　　　　　　　　　HELEN A. KELLER.

TO REV. PHILLIPS BROOKS

South Boston, June 8, 1891.

My dear Mr. Brooks,

I send you my picture as I promised, and I hope when you look at it this summer your thoughts will fly southward to your happy little friend. I used to wish that I could see pictures with my hands as I do statues, but now I do not often think about it because my dear Father has filled my mind with beautiful pictures, even of things I cannot see. If the light were not in your eyes, dear Mr. Brooks, you would understand better how happy your little Helen was when her teacher explained to her that the best and most beautiful things in the world cannot be seen nor even touched, but just felt in the heart. Every day I find out something which makes me glad. Yesterday I thought for the first time what a beautiful thing motion was, and it seemed to me that everything was trying to get

near to God, does it seem that way to you? It is
Sunday morning, and while I sit here in the library
writing this letter you are teaching hundreds of people
some of the grand and beautiful things about their
heavenly Father. Are you not very, very happy? and
when you are a Bishop you will preach to more people
and more and more will be made glad. Teacher sends
her kind remembrances, and I send you with my
picture my dear love.

> From your little friend
> HELEN A. KELLER.

When the Perkins Institution closed in June, Helen and her
teacher went south to Tuscumbia, where they remained until
December. There is a hiatus of several months in the letters
caused by the depressing effect on Helen and Miss Sullivan of
the "Frost King" episode. At the time this trouble seemed very
grave and brought them much unhappiness. An analysis of the
case has been made elsewhere, and Miss Keller has written
her account of it.*

TO MR. ALBERT H. MUNSELL

Brewster, Mar. 10, 1892.

My dear Mr. Munsell,
Surely I need not tell you that your letter was very
welcome. I enjoyed every word of it and wished that it
was longer. I laughed when you spoke of old Neptune's
wild moods. He has, in truth, behaved very strangely
ever since we came to Brewster. It is evident that
something has displeased his Majesty but I cannot
imagine what it can be. His expression has been so
turbulent that I have feared to give him your kind
message. Who knows! Perhaps the Old Sea God as he
lay asleep upon the shore, heard the soft music of

* Pages 44–51

growing things—the stir of life in the earth's bosom,
and his stormy heart was angry, because he knew that
his and Winter's reign was almost at an end. So together
the unhappy monarch[s] fought most despairingly,
thinking that gentle Spring would turn and fly at the
very sight of the havoc caused by their forces. But lo!
the lovely maiden only smiles more sweetly, and
breathes upon the icy battlements of her enemies, and
in a moment they vanish, and the glad Earth gives her a
royal welcome. But I must put away these idle fancies
until we meet again. Please give your dear mother my
love. Teacher wishes me to say that she liked the
photograph very much and she will see about having
some when we return. Now, dear friend, please accept
these few words because of the love that is linked with
them.

> Lovingly yours
> HELEN A. KELLER.

This letter was reproduced in facsimile in *St. Nicholas*, June,
1892. It is undated, but must have been written two or three
months before it was published.

TO *St. Nicholas*

Dear St. Nicholas:
It gives me very great pleasure to send you my
autograph because I want the boys and girls who read
St. Nicholas to know how blind children write. I
suppose some of them wonder how we keep the lines
so straight so I will try to tell them how it is done. We
have a grooved board which we put between the pages
when we wish to write. The parallel grooves
correspond to lines and when we have pressed the
paper into them by means of the blunt end of the pencil
it is very easy to keep the words even. The small letters
are all made in the grooves, while the long ones extend

above and below them. We guide the pencil with the
right hand, and feel carefully with the forefinger of the
left hand to see that we shape and space the letters
correctly. It is very difficult at first to form them
plainly, but if we keep on trying it gradually becomes
easier, and after a great deal of practice we can write
legible letters to our friends. Then we are very, very
happy. Sometime they may visit a school for the blind.
If they do, I am sure they will wish to see the pupils
write.

Very sincerely your little friend
HELEN A. KELLER.

In May, 1892, Helen gave a tea in aid of the kindergarten for
the blind. It was quite her own idea, and was given in the
house of Mrs. Mahlon D. Spaulding, sister of Mr. John P.
Spaulding, one of Helen's kindest and most liberal friends.
The tea brought more than two thousand dollars for the blind
children.

TO MISS CAROLINE DERBY

South Boston, May 9, 1892.

My dear Miss Carrie:—I was much pleased to receive
your kind letter. Need I tell you that I was more than
delighted to hear that you are really interested in the
"tea"? Of course we must not give it up. Very soon I am
going far away, to my own dear home, in the sunny
south, and it would always make me happy to think that
the last thing which my dear friends in Boston did for
my pleasure was to help make the lives of many little
sightless children good and happy. I know that kind
people cannot help feeling a tender sympathy for the
little ones, who cannot see the beautiful light, or any of
the wonderful things which give them pleasure; and it
seems to me that all loving sympathy must express
itself in acts of kindness; and when the friends of little

helpless blind children understand that we are working
for their happiness, they will come and make our "tea"
a success, and I am sure I shall be the happiest little girl
in all the world. Please let Bishop Brooks know our
plans, so that he may arrange to be with us. I am glad
Miss Eleanor is interested. Please give her my love. I
will see you tomorrow and then we can make the rest of
our plans. Please give your dear aunt teacher's and my
love and tell her that we enjoyed our little visit very
much indeed.

Lovingly yours,
HELEN A. KELLER.

TO MR. JOHN P. SPAULDING

South Boston, May 11th, 1892.

My dear Mr. Spaulding:—I am afraid you will think
your little friend, Helen, very troublesome when you
read this letter; but I am sure you will not blame me
when I tell you that I am very anxious about something.
You remember teacher and I told you Sunday that I
wanted to have a little tea in aid of the kindergarten. We
thought everything was arranged: but we found
Monday that Mrs. Elliott would not be willing to let us
invite more than fifty people, because Mrs. Howe's
house is quite small. I am sure that a great many people
would like to come to the tea, and help me do
something to brighten the lives of little blind children;
but some of my friends say that I shall have to give up
the idea of having a tea unless we can find another
house. Teacher said yesterday, that perhaps Mrs.
Spaulding would be willing to let us have her beautiful
house, and [I] thought I would ask you about it. Do you
think Mrs. Spaulding would help me, if I wrote to her? I
shall be so disappointed if my little plans fail, because I
have wanted for a long time to do something for the

poor little ones who are waiting to enter the kindergarten. Please let me know what you think about the house, and try to forgive me for troubling you so much.

Lovingly your little friend,
HELEN A. KELLER.

TO MR. EDWARD H. CLEMENT

South Boston, May 18th, 1892.

My dear Mr. Clement:—I am going to write to you this beautiful morning because my heart is brimful of happiness and I want you and all my dear friends in the *Transcript* office to rejoice with me. The preparations for my tea are nearly completed, and I am looking forward joyfully to the event. I know I shall not fail. Kind people will not disappoint me, when they know that I plead for helpless little children who live in darkness and ignorance. They will come to my tea and buy light,—the beautiful light of knowledge and love for many little ones who are blind and friendless. I remember perfectly when my dear teacher came to me. Then I was like the little blind children who are waiting to enter the kindergarten. There was no light in my soul. This wonderful world with all its sunlight and beauty was hidden from me, and I had never dreamed of its loveliness. But teacher came to me and taught my little fingers to use the beautiful key that has unlocked the door of my dark prison and set my spirit free.

It is my earnest wish to share my happiness with others, and I ask the kind people of Boston to help me make the lives of little blind children brighter and happier.

Lovingly your little friend,
HELEN A. KELLER.

At the end of June Miss Sullivan and Helen went home to Tuscumbia.

TO MISS CAROLINE DERBY

Tuscumbia, Alabama, July 9th 1892.

My dear Carrie—You are to look upon it as a most positive proof of my love that I write to you to-day. For a whole week it has been "cold and dark and dreary" in Tuscumbia, and I must confess the continuous rain and dismalness of the weather fills me with gloomy thoughts and makes the writing of letters, or any pleasant employment, seem quite impossible. Nevertheless, I must tell you that we are alive,—that we reached home safely, and that we speak of you daily, and enjoy your interesting letters very much. I had a beautiful visit at Hulton. Everything was fresh and spring-like, and we stayed out of doors all day. We even ate our breakfast out on the piazza. Sometimes we sat in the hammock, and teacher read to me. I rode horseback nearly every evening and once I rode five miles at a fast gallop. O, it was great fun! Do you like to ride? I have a very pretty little cart now, and if it ever stops raining teacher and I are going to drive every evening. And I have another beautiful Mastiff— the largest one I ever saw—and he will go along to protect us. His name is Eumer. A queer name, is it not? I think it is Saxon. We expect to go to the mountains next week. My little brother, Phillips, is not well, and we think the clear mountain air will benefit him. Mildred is a sweet little sister and I am sure you would love her. I thank you very much for your photograph. I like to have my friends' pictures even though I cannot see them. I was greatly amused at the idea of your writing the square hand. I do not write on a Braille tablet, as you suppose, but on a grooved board like the piece which I enclose. You could not read

Braille; for it is written in dots, not at all like ordinary
letters. Please give my love to Miss Derby and tell her
that I hope she gave my sweetest love to Baby Ruth.
What was the book you sent me for my birthday? I
received several, and I do not know which was from
you. I had one gift which especially pleased me. It was
a lovely cape crocheted, for me, by an old gentleman,
seventy-five years of age. And every stitch, he writes,
represents a kind wish for my health and happiness. Tell
your little cousins I think they had better get upon the
fence with me until after the election; for there are so
many parties and candidates that I doubt if such
youthful politicians would make a wise selection.
Please give my love to Rosy when you write, and
believe me,

> YOUR LOVING FRIEND
> HELEN A. KELLER.

P.S. How do you like this type-written letter?

> H.K.

TO MRS. GROVER CLEVELAND

My dear Mrs. Cleveland,
I am going to write you a little letter this beautiful
morning because I love you and dear little Ruth very
much indeed, and also because I wish to thank you for
the loving message which you sent me through Miss
Derby. I am glad, very glad that such a kind, beautiful
lady loves me. I have loved you for a long time, but I
did not think you had ever heard of me until your
sweet message came. Please kiss your dear little baby
for me, and tell her I have a little brother nearly
sixteen months old. His name is Phillips Brooks. I
named him myself after my dear friend Phillips
Brooks. I send you with this letter a pretty book which
my teacher thinks will interest you, and my picture.

Please accept them with the love and good wishes of
your friend,

HELEN A. KELLER.

Tuscumbia, Alabama.
November fourth. [1892.]

Hitherto the letters have been given in full; from this point on
passages are omitted and the omissions are indicated.

TO MR. JOHN HITZ

Tuscumbia, Alabama, Dec. 19, 1892.

My Dear Mr. Hitz,

I hardly know how to begin a letter to you, it has been
such a long time since your kind letter reached me, and
there is so much that I would like to write if I could.
You must have wondered why your letter has not had
an answer, and perhaps you have thought Teacher and
me very naughty indeed. If so, you will be very sorry
when I tell you something. Teacher's eyes have been
hurting her so that she could not write to any one, and
I have been trying to fulfil a promise which I made last
summer. Before I left Boston, I was asked to write a
sketch of my life for the *Youth's Companion*. I had
intended to write the sketch during my vacation: but I
was not well, and I did not feel able to write even to
my friends. But when the bright, pleasant autumn days
came, and I felt strong again I began to think about the
sketch. It was some time before I could plan it to suit
me. You see, it is not very pleasant to write all about
one's self. At last, however, I got something bit by bit
that Teacher thought would do, and I set about putting
the scraps together, which was not an easy task: for,
although I worked some on it every day, I did not finish
it until a week ago Saturday. I sent the sketch to the
Companion as soon as it was finished; but I do not

know that they will accept it. Since then, I have not
been well, and I have been obliged to keep very quiet,
and rest; but to-day I am better, and to-morrow I shall
be well again, I hope.

The reports which you have read in the paper about
me are not true at all. We received the *Silent Worker*
which you sent, and I wrote right away to the editor to
tell him that it was a mistake. Sometimes I am not
well; but I am not a "wreck," and there is nothing
"distressing" about my condition.

I enjoyed your dear letter so much! I am always
delighted when anyone writes me a beautiful thought
which I can treasure in my memory forever. It is
because my books are full of the riches of which Mr.
Ruskin speaks that I love them so dearly. I did not
realize until I began to write the sketch for the
Companion, what precious companions books have
been to me, and how blessed even my life has been:
and now I am happier than ever because I do realize
the happiness that has come to me. I hope you will
write to me as often as you can. Teacher and I are
always delighted to hear from you. I want to write to
Mr. Bell and send him my picture. I suppose he has
been too busy to write to his little friend. I often think
of the pleasant time we had all together in Boston last
spring.

Now I am going to tell you a secret. I think we,
Teacher, and my father and little sister, and myself,
will visit Washington next March!!! Then I shall see
you, and dear Mr. Bell, and Elsie and Daisy again!
Would not it be lovely if Mrs. Pratt could meet us
there? I think I will write to her and tell her the secret
too....

LOVINGLY YOUR LITTLE FRIEND,
HELEN A. KELLER.

P.S. Teacher says you want to know what kind of a
pet I would like to have. I love all living things,—I

suppose everyone does; but of course I cannot have a
menagerie. I have a beautiful pony, and a large dog.
And I would like a little dog to hold in my lap, or a big
pussy (there are no fine cats in Tuscumbia) or a parrot.
I would like to feel a parrot talk, it would be so much
fun! but I would be pleased with, and love any little
creature you send me.

H.K.

TO MISS CAROLINE DERBY

Tuscumbia, Alabama, February 18, 1893.
... You have often been in my thoughts during these
sad days, while my heart has been grieving over the
loss of my beloved friend,* and I have wished many
times that I was in Boston with those who knew and
loved him as I did ... he was so much of a friend to
me! so tender and loving always! I do try not to mourn
his death too sadly. I do try to think that he is still
near, very near; but sometimes the thought that he is
not here, that I shall not see him when I go to
Boston,—that he is gone,—rushes over my soul like a
great wave of sorrow. But at other times, when I am
happier, I do feel his beautiful presence, and his
loving hand leading me in pleasant ways. Do you
remember the happy hour we spent with him last June
when he held my hand, as he always did, and talked to
us about his friend Tennyson, and our own dear poet
Dr. Holmes, and I tried to teach him the manual
alphabet, and he laughed so gaily over his mistakes,
and afterward I told him about my tea, and he
promised to come? I can hear him now, saying in his
cheerful, decided way, in reply to my wish that my tea
might be a success, "Of course it will, Helen. Put your
whole heart in the good work, my child, and it cannot

---

* Phillips Brooks died January 23, 1893.

fail." I am glad the people are going to raise a
monument to his memory. . . .

In March Helen and Miss Sullivan went North, and spent the
next few months traveling and visiting friends.

In reading this letter about Niagara one should remember
that Miss Keller knows distance and shape, and that the size
of Niagara is within her experience after she has explored
it, crossed the bridge and gone down in the elevator. Especially important are such details as her feeling the rush of the
water by putting her hand on the window. Dr. Bell gave her a
down pillow, which she held against her to increase the vibrations.

TO MRS. KATE ADAMS KELLER

South Boston, April 13, 1893.

. . . Teacher, Mrs. Pratt and I very unexpectedly
decided to take a journey with dear Dr. Bell Mr.
Westervelt, a gentleman whom father met in
Washington, has a school for the deaf in Rochester.
We went there first. . . .

Mr. Westervelt gave us a reception one afternoon.
A great many people came. Some of them asked odd
questions. A lady seemed surprised that I loved
flowers when I could not see their beautiful colors,
and when I assured her I did love them, she said,
"no doubt you feel the colors with your fingers." But
of course, it is not alone for their bright colors that
we love the flowers. . . . A gentleman asked me
what *beauty* meant to my mind. I must confess I
was puzzled at first. But after a minute I answered that
beauty was a form of goodness—and he went
away.

When the reception was over we went back to the
hotel and teacher slept quite unconscious of the
surprise which was in store for her. Mr. Bell and I

planned it together, and Mr. Bell made all the
arrangements before we told teacher anything about it.
This was the surprise—I was to have the pleasure of
taking my dear teacher to see Niagara Falls! . . .

The hotel was so near the river that I could feel it
rushing past by putting my hand on the window. The
next morning the sun rose bright and warm, and we
got up quickly for our hearts were full of pleasant
expectation. . . . You can never imagine how I felt when
I stood in the presence of Niagara until you have the
same mysterious sensations yourself. I could hardly
realize that it was water that I felt rushing and
plunging with impetuous fury at my feet. It seemed
as if it were some living thing rushing on to some
terrible fate. I wish I could describe the cataract as it
is, its beauty and awful grandeur, and the fearful and
irresistible plunge of its waters over the brow of the
precipice. One feels helpless and overwhelmed in the
presence of such a vast force. I had the same feeling
once before when I first stood by the great ocean and
felt its waves beating against the shore. I suppose
you feel so, too, when you gaze up to the stars in the
stillness of the night, do you not? . . . We went down
a hundred and twenty feet in an elevator that we might
see the violent eddies and whirlpools in the deep
gorge below the Falls. Within two miles of the Falls
is a wonderful suspension bridge. It is thrown across
the gorge at a height of two hundred and fifty-eight
feet above the water and is supported on each bank by
towers of solid rock, which are eight hundred feet
apart. When we crossed over to the Canadian side, I
cried, "God save the Queen!" Teacher said I was a
little traitor. But I do not think so. I was only doing as
the Canadians do, while I was in their country, and
besides I honor England's good queen.

You will be pleased, dear Mother, to hear that a
kind lady whose name is Miss Hooker is endeavoring

to improve my speech. Oh, I do so hope and pray that
I shall speak well some day! ...

Mr. Munsell spent last Sunday evening with us.
How you would have enjoyed hearing him tell about
Venice! His beautiful word-pictures made us feel as if
[we] were sitting in the shadow of San Marco,
dreaming, or sailing upon the moonlit canal.... I hope
when I visit Venice, as I surely shall some day, that
Mr. Munsell will go with me. That is my castle in the
air. You see, none of my friends describe things to me
so vividly and so beautifully as he does....

Her visit to the World's Fair she described in a letter to Mr.
John P. Spaulding, which was published in *St. Nicholas*, and is
much like the following letter. In a prefatory note which Miss
Sullivan wrote for *St. Nicholas*, she says that people frequently said to her, "Helen sees more with her fingers than we
do with our eyes." The President of the Exposition gave her
this letter:

TO THE CHIEFS OF THE DEPARTMENTS AND OFFICERS IN CHARGE OF BUILDINGS AND EXHIBITS

Gentlemen—The bearer, Miss Helen Keller,
accompanied by Miss Sullivan, is desirous of making a
complete inspection of the Exposition in all
Departments. She is blind and deaf, but is able to
converse, and is introduced to me as one having a
wonderful ability to understand the objects she visits,
and as being possessed of a high order of intelligence
and of culture beyond her years. Please favour her with
every facility to examine the exhibits in the several
Departments, and extend to her such other courtesies
as may be possible.

Thanking you in advance for the same, I am, with respect,

> Very truly yours,
> (SIGNED) H. N. HIGINBOTHAM,
> PRESIDENT.

TO MISS CAROLINE DERBY

Hulton, Penn., August 17, 1893.

... Every one at the Fair was very kind to me....
Nearly all of the exhibitors seemed perfectly willing
to let me touch the most delicate things, and they were
very nice about explaining everything to me. A French
gentleman, whose name I cannot remember, showed
me the great French bronzes. I believe they gave me
more pleasure than anything else at the Fair: they were
so lifelike and wonderful to my touch. Dr. Bell went
with us himself to the electrical building, and showed
us some of the historical telephones. I saw the one
through which Emperor Dom Pedro listened to the
words, "To be, or not to be," at the Centenial. Dr.
Gillett of Illinois took us to the Liberal Arts and
Woman's buildings. In the former I visited Tiffany's
exhibit, and held the beautiful Tiffany diamond,
which is valued at one hundred thousand dollars, and
touched many other rare and costly things. I sat in
King Ludwig's armchair and felt like a queen when
Dr. Gillett remarked that I had many loyal subjects.
At the Woman's building we met the Princess Maria
Schaovskoy of Russia, and a beautiful Syrian lady. I
liked them both very much. I went to the Japanese
department with Prof. Morse who is a well-known
lecturer. I never realized what a wonderful people the
Japanese are until I saw their most interesting exhibit.
Japan must indeed be a paradise for children to
judge from the great number of playthings which are

manufactured there. The queer-looking Japanese
musical instruments, and their beautiful works of
art were interesting. The Japanese books are very odd.
There are forty-seven letters in their alphabets.
Prof. Morse knows a great deal about Japan, and is
very kind and wise. He invited me to visit his
museum in Salem the next time I go to Boston. But I
think I enjoyed the sails on the tranquil lagoon, and
the lovely scenes, as my friends described them to me,
more than anything else at the Fair. Once, while we
were out on the water, the sun went down over the rim
of the earth, and threw a soft, rosy light over the
White City, making it look more than ever like
Dreamland. . . .

Of course, we visited the Midway Plaisance. It was
a bewildering and fascinating place. I went into the
streets of Cairo, and rode on the camel. That was fine
fun. We also rode in the Ferris wheel, and on the ice-
railway, and had a sail in the Whaleback. . . .

In the spring of 1893 a club was started in Tuscumbia, of
which Mrs. Keller was president, to establish a public library.
Miss Keller says:

"I wrote to my friends about the work and enlisted their
sympathy. Several hundred books, including many fine ones,
were sent to me in a short time, as well as money and encouragement. This generous assistance encouraged the ladies, and
they have gone on collecting and buying books ever since, until now they have a very respectable public library in the
town."

TO MRS. CHARLES E. INCHES

Hulton, Penn., Oct. 21, 1893.

. . . We spent September at home in Tuscumbia . . . and
were all very happy together. . . . Our quiet mountain
home was especially attractive and restful after the

excitement and fatigue of our visit to the World's Fair. We enjoyed the beauty and solitude of the hills more than ever.

And now we are in Hulton, Penn. again where I am going to study this winter with a tutor assisted by my dear teacher. I study Arithmetic, Latin and literature. I enjoy my lessons very much. It is so pleasant to learn about new things. Every day I find how little I know, but I do not feel discouraged since God has given me an eternity in which to learn more. In literature I am studying Longfellow's poetry. I know a great deal of it by heart, for I loved it long before I knew a metaphor from a synecdoche. I used to say I did not like arithmetic very well, but now I have changed my mind. I see what a good and useful study it is, though I must confess my mind wanders from it sometimes! for, nice and useful as arithmetic is, it is not as interesting as a beautiful poem or a lovely story. But bless me, how time does fly. I have only a few moments left in which to answer your questions about the "Helen Keller" Public Library.

1. I think there are about 3,000 people in Tuscumbia, Ala., and perhaps half of them are colored people. 2. At present there is no library of any sort in the town. That is why I thought about starting one. My mother and several of my lady friends said they would help me, and they formed a club, the object of which is to work for the establishment of a free public library in Tuscumbia. They have now about 100 books and about $55 in money, and a kind gentleman has given us land on which to erect a library building. But in the meantime the club has rented a little room in a central part of the town, and the books which we already have are free to all. 3. Only a few of my kind friends in Boston know anything about the library. I did not like to trouble them while I was trying to get money for poor little Tommy; for of course it was more important that he should be educated than that my people should have books to read.

4. I do not know what books we have, but I think it is a miscellaneous (I think that is the word) collection....

P. S. My teacher thinks it would be more business-like to say that a list of the contributors toward the building fund will be kept and published in my father's paper, the "North Alabamian."

H. K.

TO MISS CAROLINE DERBY

Hulton, Penn., December 28, 1893.

...Please thank dear Miss Derby for me for the pretty shield which she sent me. It is a very interesting souvenir of Columbus, and of the Fair White City; but I cannot imagine what discoveries I have made,—I mean new discoveries. We are all discoverers in one sense, being born quite ignorant of all things; but I hardly think that is what she meant. Tell her she must explain why I am a discoverer....

TO DR. EDWARD EVERETT HALE

Hulton, Pennsylvania, January 14, (1894).

My dear Cousin: I had thought to write to you long before this in answer to your kind letter which I was so glad to receive, and to thank you for the beautiful little book which you sent me; but I have been very busy since the beginning of the New Year. The publication of my little story in the *Youth's Companion* has brought me a large number of letters,—last week I received sixty-one!—and besides replying to some of these letters, I have many lessons to learn, among them Arithmetic and Latin; and, you know, Cæsar is Cæsar still, imperious and tyrannical, and if a little girl would understand so great a man, and the wars and conquests of which he tells in his beautiful Latin language, she

must study much and think much, and study and
thought require time.

I shall prize the little book always, not only for its
own value; but because of its associations with you.
It is a delight to think of you as the giver of one of
your books into which, I am sure, you have wrought
your own thoughts and feelings, and I thank you
very much for remembering me in such a very
beautiful way. . . .

In February Helen and Miss Sullivan returned to Tuscumbia.
They spend the rest of the spring reading and studying. In the
summer they attended the meeting at Chautauqua of the
American Association for the Promotion of the Teaching of
Speech to the Deaf, where Miss Sullivan read a paper on
Helen Keller's education.

In the fall Helen and Miss Sullivan entered the Wright-
Humason School in New York, which makes a specialty of
lip-reading and voice-culture. The "singing lessons" were to
strengthen her voice. She had taken a few piano lessons at the
Perkins Institution. The experiment was interesting, but of
course came to little.

TO MISS CAROLINE DERBY

The Wright-Humason School.
42 West 76th St.
New York, Oct. 23, 1894.

. . . The school is very pleasant, and bless you! it is
quite fashionable. . . . I study Arithmetic, English
Literature and United States History as I did last
winter. I also keep a diary. I enjoy my singing lessons
with Dr. Humason more than I can say. I expect to take
piano lessons sometime. . . .

Last Saturday our kind teachers planned a delightful
trip to Bedloe's Island to see Bartholdi's great statue of
Liberty enlightening the world. . . . The ancient cannon,

which look seaward, wear a very menacing expression;
but I doubt if there is any unkindness in their rusty old
hearts.

Liberty is a gigantic figure of a woman in Greek
draperies, holding in her right hand a torch. ... A spiral
stairway leads from the base of this pedestal to the
torch. We climbed up to the head which will hold forty
persons, and viewed the scene on which Liberty gazes
day and night, and O, how wonderful it was! We did
not wonder that the great French artist thought the
place worthy to be the home of his grand ideal. The
glorious bay lay calm and beautiful in the October
sunshine, and the ships came and went like idle
dreams; those seaward going slowly disappeared like
clouds that change from gold to gray; those homeward
coming sped more quickly like birds that seek their
mother's nest. ...

TO MISS CAROLINE DERBY

*The Wright-Humason School.
New York, March 15, 1895.*

... I think I have improved a little in lip-reading,
though I still find it very difficult to read rapid speech;
but I am sure I shall succeed some day if I only
persevere. Dr. Humason is still trying to improve my
speech. Oh, Carrie, how I should like to speak like
other people! I should be willing to work night and
day if it could only be accomplished. Think what a joy
it would be to all of my friends to hear me speak
naturally!! I wonder why it is so difficult and
perplexing for a deaf child to learn to speak when it is
so easy for other people; but I am sure I shall speak
perfectly some time if I am only patient. ...

Although I have been so busy, I have found time to
read a good deal. ... I have lately read "Wilhelm Tell"
by Schiller, and "The Lost Vestal." ... Now I am

reading "Nathan the Wise" by Lessing and "King Arthur" by Miss Mulock.

... You know our kind teachers take us to see everything which they think will interest us, and we learn a great deal in that delightful way. On George Washington's birthday we all went to the Dog Show, and although there was a great crowd in the Madison Square Garden, and despite the bewilderment caused by the variety of sounds made by the dog-orchestra, which was very confusing to those who could hear them, we enjoyed the afternoon very much. Among the dogs which received the most attention were the bull-dogs. They permitted themselves startling liberties when any one caressed them, crowding themselves almost into one's arms and helping themselves without ceremony to kisses, apparently unconscious of the impropriety of their conduct. Dear me, what unbeautiful little beasts they are! But they are so good natured and friendly, one cannot help liking them.

Dr. Humason, Teacher, and I left the others at the Dog Show and went to a reception given by the "Metropolitan Club." ... It is sometimes called the "Millionaires' Club." The building is magnificent, being built of white marble; the rooms are large and splendidly furnished; but I must confess, so much splendor is rather oppressive to me; and I didn't envy the millionaires in the least all the happiness their gorgeous surroundings are supposed to bring them....

TO MRS. KATE ADAMS KELLER

New York, March 31, 1895.
... Teacher and I spent the afternoon at Mr. Hutton's, and had a most delightful time! ... We met Mr. Clemens and Mr. Howells there! I had known about

them for a long time; but I had never thought that I
should see them, and talk to them; and I can scarcely
realize now that this great pleasure has been mine!
But, much as I wonder that I, only a little girl of
fourteen, should come in contact with so many
distinguished people, I do realize that I am a very
happy child, and very grateful for the many beautiful
privileges I have enjoyed. The two distinguished
authors were very gentle and kind, and I could not tell
which of them I loved best. Mr. Clemens told us many
entertaining stories, and made us laugh till we cried. I
only wish you could have seen and heard him! He told
us that he would go to Europe in a few days to bring
his wife and his daughter, Jeanne, back to America,
because Jeanne, who is studying in Paris, has learned
so much in three years and a half that if he did not
bring her home, she would soon know more than he
did. I think Mark Twain is a very appropriate *nom de
plume* for Mr. Clemens because it has a funny and
quaint sound, and goes well with his amusing
writings, and its nautical significance suggests the
deep and beautiful things that he has written. I think
he is very handsome indeed.... Teacher said she
thought he looked something like Paradeuski. (If that
is the way to spell the name.) Mr. Howells told me a
little about Venice, which is one of his favorite cities,
and spoke very tenderly of his dear little girl,
Winnifred, who is now with God. He has another
daughter, named Mildred, who knows Carrie. I might
have seen Mrs. Wiggin, the sweet author of "Birds'
Christmas Carol," but she had a dangerous cough and
could not come. I was much disappointed not to see
her; but I hope I shall have that pleasure some other
time. Mr. Hutton gave me a lovely little glass, shaped
like a thistle, which belonged to his dear mother, as a
souvenir of my delightful visit. We also met Mr.

Rogers . . . who kindly left his carriage to bring us home.

When the Wright-Humason School closed for the summer, Miss Sullivan and Helen went South.

TO MRS. LAURENCE HUTTON

Tuscumbia, Alabama, July 29, 1895.

. . . I am spending my vacation very quietly and pleasantly at my beautiful, sunny home, with my loving parents, my darling little sister and my small brother, Phillips. My precious teacher is with me too, and so of course I am happy I read a little, walk a little, write a little and play with the children a great deal, and the days slip by delightfully! . . .

My friends are so pleased with the improvement which I had in speech and lip-reading last year, that it has been decided best for me to continue my studies in New York another year I am delighted at the prospect of spending another year in your great city I used to think that I should never feel "at home" in New York; but since I have made the acquaintance of so many people, and can look back to such a bright and successful winter there, I find myself looking forward to next year, and anticipating still brighter and better times in the Metropolis.

Please give my kindest love to Mr Hutton, and Mrs Riggs and Mr Warner too, although I have never had the pleasure of knowing him personally. As I listen Venicewards, I hear Mr Hutton's pen dancing over the pages of his new book It is a pleasant sound because it is full of promise How much I shall enjoy reading it!

Please pardon me, my dear Mrs Hutton, for sending you a typewritten letter across the ocean I have tried several times to write with a pencil on my little writing machine since I came home; but I have found it very

difficult to do so on account of the heat The moisture
of my hand soils and blurs the paper so dreadfully, that
I am compelled to use my typewriter altogether And it
is not my "Remington" either, but a naughty little thing
that gets out of order on the slightest provocation, and
cannot be induced to make a period...

TO MRS. WILLIAM THAW

New York, October 16, 1895.

Here we are once more in the great metropolis! We
left Hulton Friday night and arrived here Saturday
morning. Our friends were greatly surprised to see us,
as they had not expected us before the last of this
month. I rested Saturday afternoon, for I was very
tired, and Sunday I visited with my schoolmates, and
now that I feel quite rested, I am going to write to you;
for I know you will want to hear that we reached New
York safely. We had to change cars at Philadelphia;
but we did not mind it much. After we had had our
breakfast, Teacher asked one of the train-men in the
station if the New York train was made up. He said no,
it would not be called for about fifteen minutes; so we
sat down to wait; but in a moment the man came back
and asked Teacher if we would like to go to the train at
once. She said we would, and he took us way out on
the track and put us on board our train. Thus we
avoided the rush and had a nice quiet visit before the
train started. Was that not very kind? So it always is.
Some one is ever ready to scatter little acts of
kindness along our pathway, making it smooth and
pleasant...

We had a quiet but very pleasant time in Hulton.
Mr. Wade is just as dear and good as ever! He has
lately had several books printed in England for me,
"Old Mortality," "The Castle of Otranto" and "King of
No-land."...

TO MISS CAROLINE DERBY

New York, December 29, 1895.

... Teacher and I have been very gay of late. We have
seen our kind friends, Mrs. Dodge, Mr. and Mrs.
Hutton, Mrs. Riggs and her husband, and met many
distinguished people, among whom were Miss Ellen
Terry, Sir Henry Irving and Mr. Stockton! Weren't we
very fortunate? Miss Terry was lovely. She kissed
Teacher and said, "I do not know whether I am glad to
see you or not; for I feel so ashamed of myself when I
think of how much you have done for the little girl."
We also met Mr. and Mrs. Terry, Miss Terry's brother
and his wife. I thought her beauty angellic, and oh,
what a clear, beautiful voice she had! We saw Miss
Terry again with Sir Henry in "King Charles the
First," a week ago last Friday, and after the play they
kindly let me feel of them and get an idea of how they
looked. How noble and kingly the King was,
especially in his misfortunes! And how pretty and
faithful the poor Queen was! The play seemed so real,
we almost forgot where we were, and believed we
were watching the genuine scenes as they were acted
so long ago. The last act affected us most deeply, and
we all wept, wondering how the executioner could
have the heart to tear the King from his loving wife's
arms.

I have just finished reading "Ivanhoe." It was very
exciting; but I must say I did not enjoy it very much.
Sweet Rebecca, with her strong, brave spirit and her
pure, generous nature, was the only character which
thoroughly won my admiration. Now I am reading
"Stories from Scottish History," and they are very
thrilling and absorbing! ...

The next two letters were written just after the death of Mr.
John P. Spaulding.

TO MRS. GEORGE H. BRADFORD

New York, February 4, 1896.

What can I say which will make you understand how
much Teacher and I appreciate your thoughtful
kindness in sending us those little souvenirs of the
dear room where we first met the best and kindest of
friends? Indeed, you can never know all the comfort
you have given us. We have put the dear picture on the
mantelpiece in our room where we can see it every
day, and I often go and touch it, and somehow I
cannot help feeling that our beloved friend is very
near to me.... It was very hard to take up our school
work again, as if nothing had happened; but I am sure
it is well that we have duties which must be done, and
which take our minds away for a time at least from our
sorrow....

TO MISS CAROLINE DERBY

New York, March 2nd, 1896.

... We miss dear King John sadly. It was so hard to
lose him, he was the best and kindest of friends, and I
do not know what we shall do without him.

We went to a poultry-show ... and the man there
kindly permitted us to feel of the birds. They were so
tame, they stood perfectly still when I handled them. I
saw great big turkeys, geese, guineas, ducks and many
others.

Almost two weeks ago we called at Mr. Hutton's
and had a delightful time. We always do! We met Mr.
Warner, the writer, Mr. Mabie, the editor of the
Outlook and other pleasant people. I am sure you
would like to know Mr. and Mrs. Hutton, they are so
kind and interesting. I can never tell you how much
pleasure they have given us.

Mr. Warner and Mr. Burroughs, the great lover of

nature, came to see us a few days after, and we had a
delightful talk with them. They were both very, very
dear! Mr. Burroughs told me about his home near the
Hudson, and what a happy place it must be! I hope we
shall visit it some day. Teacher has read me his lively
stories about his boyhood, and I enjoyed them greatly.
Have you read the beautiful poem, "Waiting"? I know
it, and it makes me feel so happy, it has such sweet
thoughts. Mr. Warner showed me a scarf-pin with a
beetle on it which was made in Egypt fifteen hundred
years before Christ, and told me that the beetle meant
immortality to the Egyptians because it wrapped itself
up and went to sleep and came out again in a new
form, thus renewing itself.

TO MISS CAROLINE DERBY

New York, April 25, 1896.
... My studies are the same as they were when I saw
you, except that I have taken up French with a French
teacher who comes three times a week. I read her lips
almost exclusively, (she does not know the manual
alphabet) and we get on quite well. I have read "Le
Médecin Malgré Lui," a very good French comedy by
Molière, with pleasure; and they say I speak French
pretty well now, and German also. Anyway, French and
German people understand what I am trying to say, and
that is very encouraging. In voice-training I have still
the same old difficulties to contend against; and the
fulfilment of my wish to speak well seems O, so far
away! Sometimes I feel sure that I catch a faint
glimpse of the goal I am striving for; but in another
minute a bend in the road hides it from my view, and I
am again left wandering in the dark! But I try hard not
to be discouraged. Surely we shall all find at last the
ideals we are seeking....

TO MR. JOHN HITZ

Brewster, Mass. July 15, 1896.

...As to the book, I am sure I shall enjoy it very much when I am admitted, by the magic of Teacher's dear fingers, into the companionship of the two sisters who went to the Immortal Fountain.

As I sit by the window writing to you, it is so lovely to have the soft, cool breezes fan my cheek, and to feel that the hard work of last year is over! Teacher seems to feel benefitted by the change too; for she is already beginning to look like her dear old self. We only need you, dear Mr. Hitz, to complete our happiness. Teacher and Mrs. Hopkins both say you *must* come as soon as you can! We will try to make you comfortable.

Teacher and I spent nine days at Philadelphia. Have you ever been at Dr. Crouter's Institution? Mr. Howes has probably given you a full account of our doings. We were busy all the time; we attended the meetings and talked with hundreds of people, among whom were dear Dr. Bell, Mr. Banerji of Calcutta, Monsieur Magnat of Paris with whom I conversed in French exclusively, and many other distinguished persons. We had looked forward to seeing you there, and so we were greatly disappointed that you did not come. We think of you so, so often! And our hearts go out to you in tenderest sympathy; and you know better than this poor letter can tell you how happy we always are to have you with us! I made a "speech" on July eighth, telling the members of the Association what an unspeakable blessing speech has been to me, and urging them to give every little deaf child an opportunity to learn to speak. Every one said I spoke very well and intelligibly. After my little "speech," we attended a reception at which over six hundred people were present. I must confess I do not like such large receptions; the people crowd so, and we have to do so

much talking; and yet it is at receptions like the one in
Philadelphia that we often meet friends whom we
learn to love afterwards. We left the city last Thursday
night, and arrived in Brewster Friday afternoon. We
missed the Cape Cod train Friday morning, and so we
came down to Provincetown in the steamer *Longfellow,*
I am glad we did so; for it was lovely and cool on the
water, and Boston Harbor is always interesting.

We spent about three weeks in Boston, after
leaving New York, and I need not tell you we had a
most delightful time. We visited our good friends,
Mr. and Mrs. Chamberlin, at Wrentham, out in the
country, where they have a lovely home. Their house
stands near a charming lake where we went boating
and canoeing, which was great fun. We also went in
bathing several times. Mr. and Mrs. Chamberlin
celebrated the 17th of June by giving a picnic to their
literary friends. There were about forty persons
present, all of whom were writers and publishers.
Our friend, Mr. Alden, the editor of *Harper's* was
there, and of course we enjoyed his society very
much. . . .

TO CHARLES DUDLEY WARNER

Brewster, Mass., September 3, 1896.
. . . I have been meaning to write to you all summer;
there were many things I wanted to tell you, and I
thought perhaps you would like to hear about our
vacation by the seaside, and our plans for next year;
but the happy, idle days slipped away so quickly, and
there were so many pleasant things to do every
moment, that I never found time to clothe my thought
in words, and send them to you. I wonder what
becomes of lost opportunities. Perhaps our guardian
angel gathers them up as we drop them, and will give
them back to us in the beautiful sometime when we

have grown wiser, and learned how to use them rightly.
But, however this may be, I cannot now write the letter
which has lain in my thought for you so long. My heart
is too full of sadness to dwell upon the happiness the
summer has brought me. My father is dead. He died
last Saturday at my home in Tuscumbia, and I was not
there. My own dear loving father! Oh, dear friend, how
shall I ever bear it! . . .

On the first of October Miss Keller entered the Cambridge
School for Young Ladies of which Mr. Arthur Gilman is
Principal. The "examinations" mentioned in this letter were
merely tests given in the school, but as they were old Harvard
papers, it is evident that in some subjects Miss Keller was already fairly well prepared for Radcliffe.

TO MRS. LAURENCE HUTTON

37 Concord Avenue, Cambridge, Mass.
October 8, 1896.

. . . I got up early this morning, so that I could write
you a few lines. I know you want to hear how I like my
school. I do wish you could come and see for yourself
what a beautiful school it is! There are about a hundred
girls, and they are all so bright and happy; it is a joy to
be with them.

You will be glad to hear that I passed my
examinations successfully. I have been examined in
English, German, French, and Greek and Roman
history. They were the entrance examinations for
Harvard College; so I feel pleased to think I could pass
them. This year is going to be a very busy one for
Teacher and myself. I am studying Arithmetic, English
Literature, English History, German, Latin, and
advanced geography; there is a great deal of
preparatory reading required, and, as few of the books

are in raised print, poor Teacher has to spell them all
out to me; and that means hard work.

You must tell Mr. Howells when you see him, that
we are living in his house....

TO MRS. WILLIAM THAW

37 Concord Avenue, Cambridge, Mass.,
December 2, 1896.

... It takes me a long time to prepare my lessons,
because I have to have every word of them spelled out
in my hand. Not one of the textbooks which I am
obliged to use is in raised print; so of course my work
is harder than it would be if I could read my lessons
over by myself. But it is harder for Teacher than it is
for me because the strain on her poor eyes is so great,
and I cannot help worrying about them. Sometimes it
really seems as if the task which we have set ourselves
were more than we can accomplish; but at other times I
enjoy my work more than I can say.

It is such a delight to be with the other girls, and do
everything that they do. I study Latin, German,
Arithmetic and English History, all of which I enjoy
except Arithmetic. I am afraid I have not a
mathematical mind; for my figures always manage to
get into the wrong places! ...

TO MRS. LAURENCE HUTTON

Cambridge, Mass., May 3, 1897

... You know I am trying very hard to get through with
the reading for the examinations in June, and this, in
addition to my regular schoolwork keeps me awfully
busy. But Johnson, and "The Plague" and everything
else must wait a few minutes this afternoon, while I
say, thank you, my dear Mrs. Hutton. ...

...What a splendid time we had at the "Players' Club." I always thought clubs were dull, smoky places, where men talked politics, and told endless stories, all about themselves and their wonderful exploits; but now I see, I must have been quite wrong....

TO MR. JOHN HITZ

Wrentham, Mass., July 9, 1897.

...Teacher and I are going to spend the summer at Wrentham, Mass. with our friends, the Chamberlins. I think you remember Mr. Chamberlin, the "Listener" in the *Boston Transcript*. They are dear, kind people....

But I know you want to hear about my examinations. I know that you will be glad to hear that I passed all of them successfully. The subjects I offered were elementary and advanced German, French, Latin, English, and Greek and Roman History. It seems almost too good to be true, does it not? All the time I was preparing for the great ordeal, I could not suppress an inward fear and trembling lest I should fail, and now it is an unspeakable relief to know that I have passed the examinations with credit. But what I consider my crown of success is the happiness and pleasure that my victory has brought dear Teacher. Indeed, I feel that the success is hers more than mine; for she is my constant inspiration....

At the end of September Miss Sullivan and Miss Keller returned to the Cambridge School, where they remained until early December. Then the interference of Mr. Gilman resulted in Mrs. Keller's withdrawing Miss Helen and her sister, Miss Mildred, from the school. Miss Sullivan and her pupil went to Wrentham, where they worked under Mr. Merton S. Keith, an enthusiastic and skillful teacher.

TO MRS. LAURENCE HUTTON

Wrentham, February 20, 1898.

... I resumed my studies soon after your departure, and in a very little while we were working as merrily as if the dreadful experience of a month ago had been but a dream. I cannot tell you how much I enjoy the country. It is so fresh, and peaceful and free! I do think I could work all day long without feeling tired if they would let me. There are so many pleasant things to do—not always very easy things,—much of my work in Algebra and Geometry is hard: but I love it all, especially Greek. Just think, I shall soon finish my grammar! Then comes the "Iliad." What an inexpressible joy it will be to read about Achilles, and Ulysses, and Andromache and Athene, and the rest of my old friends in their own glorious language! I think Greek is the loveliest language that I know anything about. If it is true that the violin is the most perfect of musical instruments, then Greek is the violin of human thought.

We have had some splendid toboganning this month. Every morning, before lesson-time, we all go out to the steep hill on the northern shore of the lake near the house, and coast for an hour or so. Some one balances the toboggan on the very crest of the hill, while we get on, and when we are ready, off we dash down the side of the hill in a headlong rush, and, leaping a projection, plunge into a snow-drift and go skimming far across the pond at a tremendous rate!

TO MRS. LAURENCE HUTTON

(Wrentham) April 12, 1898.

... I am glad Mr. Keith is so well pleased with my progress. It is true that Algebra and Geometry are growing easier all the time, especially algebra; and I have just received books in raised print which will greatly facilitate my work....

I find I get on faster, and do better work with Mr. Keith than I did in the classes at the Cambridge School, and I think it was well that I gave up that kind of work. At any rate, I have not been idle since I left school; I have accomplished more, and been happier than I could have been there....

TO MRS. LAURENCE HUTTON

(Wrentham) May 29, 1898.

... My work goes on bravely. Each day is filled to the brim with hard study; for I am anxious to accomplish as much as possible before I put away my books for the summer vacation. You will be pleased to hear that I did three problems in Geometry yesterday without assistance. Mr. Keith and Teacher were quite enthusiastic over the achievement, and I must confess, I felt somewhat elated myself. Now I feel as if I should succeed in doing something in mathematics, although I cannot see why it is so very important to know that the lines drawn from the extremities of the base of an isosceles triangle to the middle points of the opposite sides are equal! The knowledge doesn't make life any sweeter or happier, does it? On the other hand, when we learn a new word, it is the key to untold treasures....

TO CHARLES DUDLEY WARNER

Wrentham, Mass., June 7, 1898.

I am afraid you will conclude that I am not very anxious for a tandem after all, since I have let nearly a week pass without answering your letter in regard to the kind of wheel I should like. But really, I have been so constantly occupied with my studies since we returned from New York, that I have not had time even to think of the fun it would be to have a bicycle! You see, I am anxious to accomplish as much as possible before the long summer vacation begins. I am glad, though, that it is nearly time to put away my books; for the sunshine and flowers, and the lovely lake in front of our house are doing their best to tempt me away from my Greek and Mathematics, especially from the latter! I am sure the daisies and buttercups have as little use for the science of Geometry as I, in spite of the fact that they so beautifully illustrate its principles.

But bless me, I mustn't forget the tandem! The truth is, I know very little about bicycles. I have only ridden a "sociable," which is very different from the ordinary tandem. The "sociable" is safer, perhaps, than the tandem; but it is very heavy and awkward, and has a way of taking up the greater part of the road. Besides, I have been told that "sociables" cost more than other kinds of bicycles. My teacher and other friends think I could ride a Columbia tandem in the country with perfect safety. They also think your suggestion about a fixed handlebar a good one. I ride with a divided skirt, and so does my teacher; but it would be easier for her to mount a man's wheel than for me; so, if it could be arranged to have the ladies' seat behind, I think it would be better....

TO MISS CAROLINE DERBY

Wrentham, September 11, 1898.
... I am out of doors all the time, rowing, swimming, riding and doing a multitude of other pleasant things. This morning I rode over twelve miles on my tandem! I rode on a rough road, and fell off three or four times, and am now awfully lame! But the weather and the

scenery were so beautiful, and it was such fun to go
scooting over the smoother part of the road, I didn't
mind the mishaps in the least.

I have really learned to swim and dive—after a
fashion! I can swim a little under water, and do almost
anything I like, without fear of getting drowned! Isn't
that fine? It is almost no effort for me to row around
the lake, no matter how heavy the load may be. So you
can well imagine how strong and brown I am. . . .

TO MRS. LAURENCE HUTTON

12 Newbury Street, Boston,
October 23, 1898.

This is the first opportunity I have had to write to you
since we came here last Monday. We have been in such
a whirl ever since we decided to come to Boston; it
seemed as if we should never get settled. Poor Teacher
has had her hands full, attending to movers, and
express-men, and all sorts of people. I wish it were not
such a bother to move, especially as we have to do it so
often! . . .

. . . Mr. Keith comes here at half past three every
day except Saturday. He says he prefers to come here
for the present. I am reading the "Iliad," and the
"Aeneid" and Cicero, besides doing a lot in Geometry
and Algebra. The "Iliad" is beautiful with all the truth,
and grace and simplicity of a wonderfully childlike
people while the "Aeneid" is more stately and
reserved. It is like a beautiful maiden, who always
lived in a palace, surrounded by a magnificent court;
while the "Iliad" is like a splendid youth, who has had
the earth for his playground.

The weather has been awfully dismal all the week;
but to-day is beautiful, and our room floor is flooded
with sunlight. By and by we shall take a little walk in
the Public Gardens. I wish the Wrentham woods were

round the corner! But alas! they are not, and I shall
have to content myself with a stroll in the Gardens.
Somehow, after the great fields and pastures and lofty
pinegroves of the country, they seem shut-in and
conventional. Even the trees seem citified and self-
conscious. Indeed, I doubt if they are on speaking
terms with their country cousins! Do you know, I
cannot help feeling sorry for these trees with all their
fashionable airs? They are like the people whom they
see every day, who prefer the crowded, noisy city to the
quiet and freedom of the country. They do not even
suspect how circumscribed their lives are. They look
down pityingly on the country-folk, who have never
had an opportunity "to see the great world." Oh my! if
they only realized their limitations, they would flee for
their lives to the woods and fields. But what nonsense
is this! You will think I'm pining away for my beloved
Wrentham, which is true in one sense and not in
another. I do miss Red Farm and the dear ones there
dreadfully; but I am not unhappy. I have Teacher and
my books, and I have the certainty that something
sweet and good will come to me in this great city,
where human beings struggle so bravely all their lives
to wring happiness from cruel circumstances. Anyway,
I am glad to have my share in life, whether it be bright
or sad. . . .

TO MRS. WILLIAM THAW

Boston, December 6th, 1898.

My teacher and I had a good laugh over the girls'
frolic. How funny they must have looked in their
"rough-rider" costumes, mounted upon their fiery
steeds! "Slim" would describe them, if they were
anything like the saw-horses I have seen. What jolly
times they must have at——! I cannot help wishing
sometimes that I could have some of the fun that other

girls have. How quickly I should lock up all those
mighty warriors, and hoary sages, and impossible
heroes, who are now almost my only companions; and
dance and sing and frolic like other girls! But I must
not waste my time wishing idle wishes; and after all
my ancient friends are very wise and interesting, and I
usually enjoy their society very much indeed. It is
only once in a great while that I feel discontented, and
allow myself to wish for things I cannot hope for in
this life. But, as you know, my heart is usually brimful
of happiness. The thought that my dear Heavenly
Father is always near, giving me abundantly of all
those things, which truly enrich life and make it sweet
and beautiful, makes every deprivation seem of little
moment compared with the countless blessings I
enjoy.

TO MRS. WILLIAM THAW

12 Newbury Street, Boston,
December 19th, 1898.

...I realize now what a selfish greedy girl I was to ask
that my cup of happiness should be filled to over-
flowing, without stopping to think how many other
people's cups were quite empty. I feel heartily
ashamed of my thoughtlessness. One of the childish
illusions, which it has been hardest for me to get rid
of, is that we have only to make our wishes known in
order to have them granted. But I am slowly learning
that there is not happiness enough in the world for
everyone to have all that he wants; and it grieves me
to think that I should have forgotten, even for a
moment, that I already have more than my share, and
that like poor little Oliver Twist I should have asked
for "more...."

TO MRS. LAURENCE HUTTON

12 Newbury Street, Boston,
December 22, (1898)

...I suppose Mr. Keith writes you the work-a-day news. If so, you know that I have finished all the geometry, and nearly all the Algebra required for the Harvard examinations, and after Christmas I shall begin a very careful review of both subjects. You will be glad to hear that I enjoy Mathematics now. Why, I can do long, complicated quadratic equations in my head quite easily, and it is great fun! I think Mr. Keith is a wonderful teacher, and I feel very grateful to him for having made me see the beauty of Mathematics. Next to my own dear teacher, he has done more than any one else to enrich and broaden my mind.

TO MRS. LAURENCE HUTTON

12 Newbury Street, Boston,
January 17, 1899.

...Have you seen Kipling's "Dreaming True," or "Kitchener's School?" It is a very strong poem and set me dreaming too. Of course you have read about the "Gordon Memorial College," which the English people are to erect at Khartoum. While I was thinking over the blessings that would come to the people of Egypt through this college, and eventually to England herself, there came into my heart the strong desire that my own dear country should in a similar way convert the terrible loss of her brave sons on the "Maine" into a like blessing to the people of Cuba. Would a college at Havana not be the noblest and most enduring monument that could be raised to the brave men of the "Maine," as well as a source of infinite good to all concerned? Imagine entering the Havana harbor, and having the pier, where the "Maine" was anchored on that dreadful night, when she was so mysteriously destroyed, pointed out to you, and being told that the great, beautiful building overlooking the spot was the "Maine Memorial College," erected by the American people, and having for its object the education both of Cubans and Spaniards! What a glorious triumph such a monument would be of the best and highest instincts of a Christian nation! In it there would be no suggestion of hatred or revenge, nor a trace of the old-time belief that might makes right. On the other hand, it would be a pledge to the world that we intend to stand by our declaration of war, and give Cuba to the Cubans, as soon as we have fitted them to assume the duties and responsibilities of a self-governing people....

TO MR. JOHN HITZ

12 Newbury Street, Boston,
February 3, 1899.

... I had an exceedingly interesting experience last Monday. A kind friend took me over in the morning to the Boston Art Museum. She had previously obtained permission from General Loring, Supt. of the Museum, for me to touch the statues, especially those which represented my old friends in the "Iliad" and "Aeneid." Was that not lovely? While I was there, General Loring himself came in, and showed me some of the most beautiful statues, among which were the Venus of Medici, the Minerva of the Parthenon, Diana, in her hunting costume, with her hand on the quiver and a doe by her side, and the unfortunate Laocoön and his two little sons, struggling in the fearful coils of two huge serpents, and stretching their arms to the skies with heart-rending cries. I also saw Apollo Belvidere. He had just slain the Python and

was standing by a great pillar of rock, extending his
graceful hand in triumph over the terrible snake. Oh,
he was simply beautiful! Venus entranced me. She
looked as if she had just risen from the foam of the
sea, and her loveliness was like a strain of heavenly
music. I also saw poor Niobe with her youngest child
clinging close to her while she implored the cruel
goddess not to kill her last darling. I almost cried, it
was all so real and tragic. General Loring kindly
showed me a copy of one of the wonderful bronze
doors of the Baptistry of Florence, and I felt of the
graceful pillars, resting on the backs of fierce lions.
So you see, I had a foretaste of the pleasure which I
hope some day to have of visiting Florence. My
friend said, she would sometime show me the copies
of the marbles brought away by Lord Elgin from the
Parthenon. But somehow, I should prefer to see
the originals in the place where Genius meant them
to remain, not only as a hymn of praise to the gods,
but also as a monument of the glory of Greece. It
really seems wrong to snatch such sacred things
away from the sanctuary of the Past where they
belong. . . .

TO MR. WILLIAM WADE

Boston, February 19th, 1899.

Why, bless you, I thought I wrote to you the day after
the "Eclogues" arrived, and told you how glad I was to
have them! Perhaps you never got that letter. At any
rate, I thank you, dear friend, for taking such a world
of trouble for me. You will be glad to hear that the
books from England are coming now. I already have
the seventh and eighth books of the "Aeneid" and one
book of the "Iliad," all of which is most fortunate, as I
have come almost to the end of my embossed
textbooks.

It gives me great pleasure to hear how much is being done for the deaf-blind. The more I learn of them, the more kindness I find. Why, only a little while ago people thought it quite impossible to teach the deaf-blind anything; but no sooner was it proved possible than hundreds of kind, sympathetic hearts were fired with the desire to help them, and now we see how many of those poor, unfortunate persons are being taught to see the beauty and reality of life. Love always finds its way to an imprisoned soul, and leads it out into the world of freedom and intelligence!

As to the two-handed alphabet, I think it is much easier for those who have sight than the manual alphabet; for most of the letters look like the large capitals in books; but I think when it comes to teaching a deaf-blind person to spell, the manual alphabet is much more convenient, and less conspicuous. . . .

TO MRS. LAURENCE HUTTON

12 Newberry Street, Boston,
March 5, 1899.

. . . I am now sure that I shall be ready for my examinations in June. There is but one cloud in my sky at present; but that is one which casts a dark shadow over my life, and makes me very anxious at times. My teacher's eyes are no better: indeed, I think they grow more troublesome, though she is very brave and patient, and will not give up. But it is most distressing to me to feel that she is sacrificing her sight for me. I feel as if I ought to give up the idea of going to college altogether: for not all the knowledge in the world could make me happy, if obtained at such a cost. I do wish, Mrs. Hutton, you would try to persuade Teacher to take a rest, and have her eyes treated. She will not listen to me.

I have just had some pictures taken, and if they are good, I would like to send one to Mr. Rogers, if you think he would like to have it. I would like so much to show him in some way how deeply I appreciate all that he is doing for me, and I cannot think of anything better to do.

Every one here is talking about the Sargent pictures. It is a wonderful exhibition of portraits, they say. How I wish I had eyes to see them! How I should delight in their beauty and color! However, I am glad that I am not debarred from all pleasure in the pictures. I have at least the satisfaction of seeing them through the eyes of my friends, which is a real pleasure. I am so thankful that I can rejoice in the beauties, which my friends gather and put into my hands!

We are all so glad and thankful that Mr. Kipling did not die! I have his "Jungle-Book" in raised print, and what a splendid, refreshing book it is! I cannot help feeling as if I knew its gifted author. What a real, manly, lovable nature his must be! . . .

TO DR. DAVID H. GREER

12 Newberry Street, Boston, May 8, 1899.
. . . Each day brings me all that I can possibly accomplish, and each night brings me rest, and the sweet thought that I am a little nearer to my goal than ever before. My Greek progresses finely. I have finished the ninth book of the "Iliad" and am just beginning the "Odyssey." I am also reading the "Aeneid" and the "Eclogues." Some of my friends tell me that I am very foolish to give so much time to Greek and Latin; but I am sure they would not think so, if they realized what a wonderful world of experience and thought Homer and Virgil have opened up to me. I think I shall enjoy the "Odyssey" most of

all. The "Iliad" tells of almost nothing but war, and
one sometimes wearies of the clash of spears and the
din of battle, but the "Odyssey" tells of nobler
courage—the courage of a soul sore tried, but
steadfast to the end. I often wonder, as I read these
splendid poems why, at the same time that Homer's
songs of war fired the Greeks with valor, his songs of
manly virtue did not have a stronger influence upon
the spiritual life of the people. Perhaps the reason is,
that thoughts truly great are like seeds cast into the
human mind, and either lie there unnoticed, or are
tossed about and played with, like toys, until grown
wise through suffering and experience, a race
discovers and cultivates them. Then the world has
advanced one step in its heavenward march.

I am working very hard just now. I intend to take
my examinations in June, and there is a great deal to
be done, before I shall feel ready to meet the
ordeal. . . .

You will be glad to hear that my mother, and little
sister and brother are coming north to spend this
summer with me. We shall all live together in a small
cottage on one of the lakes at Wrentham, while my
dear teacher takes a much needed rest. She has not
had a vacation for twelve years, think of it, and all that
time she has been the sunshine of my life. Now her
eyes are troubling her a great deal, and we all think
she ought to be relieved, for a while, of every care and
responsibility. But we shall not be quite separated; we
shall see each other every day, I hope. And, when July
comes, you can think of me as rowing my dear ones
around the lovely lake in the little boat you gave me,
the happiest girl in the world! . . .

TO MRS. LAURENCE HUTTON

(Boston) May 28th (1899).

... We have had a hard day. Mr. Keith was here for
three hours this afternoon, pouring a torrent of Latin
and Greek into my poor bewildered brain. I really
believe he knows more Latin and Greek Grammar than
Cicero or Homer ever dreamed of! Cicero is splendid,
but his orations are very difficult to translate. I feel
ashamed sometimes, when I make that eloquent man
say what sounds absurd or insipid; but how is a school-
girl to interpret such genius? Why, I should have to be
a Cicero to talk like a Cicero! ...

Linnie Haguewood is a deaf-blind girl, one of the many whom
Mr. William Wade has helped. She is being educated by Miss
Dora Donald who, at the beginning of her work with her pupil,
was supplied by Mr. Hitz, Superintendent of the Volta Bureau,
with copies of all documents relating to Miss Sullivan's work
with Miss Keller.

TO MR. WILLIAM WADE

Wrentham, Mass., June 5, 1899.

...Linnie Haguewood's letter, which you sent me
some weeks ago, interested me very much. It seemed
to show spontaneity and great sweetness of character.
I was a good deal amused by what she said about
history. I am sorry she does not enjoy it; but I too feel
sometimes how dark, and mysterious and even fearful
the history of old peoples, old religions and old forms
of government really is.

Well, I must confess, I do not like the sign-
language, and I do not think it would be of much use
to the deaf-blind. I find it very difficult to follow the
rapid motions made by the deaf-mutes, and besides,
signs seem a great hindrance to them in acquiring the

power of using language easily and freely. Why, I find it hard to understand them sometimes when they spell on their fingers. On the whole, if they cannot be taught articulation, the manual alphabet seems the best and most convenient means of communication. At any rate, I am sure the deaf-blind cannot learn to use signs with any degree of facility.

The other day, I met a deaf Norwegian gentleman, who knows Ragnhild Kaata and her teacher very well, and we had a very interesting conversation about her. He said she was very industrious and happy. She spins, and does a great deal of fancy work, and reads, and leads a pleasant, useful life. Just think, she cannot use the manual alphabet! She reads the lips well, and if she cannot understand a phrase, her friends write it in her hand; and in this way she converses with strangers. I cannot make out anything written in my hand, so you see, Ragnhild has got ahead of me in some things. I do hope I shall see her sometime....

TO MRS. LAURENCE HUTTON

Wrentham, July 29, 1899.

... I passed in all the subjects I offered, and with credit in advanced Latin ... But I must confess, I had a hard time on the second day of my examinations. They would not allow Teacher to read any of the papers to me; so the papers were copied for me in braille. This arrangement worked very well in the languages, but not nearly so well in the Mathematics. Consequently, I did not do so well as I should have done, if Teacher had been allowed to read the Algebra and Geometry to me. But you must not think I blame any one. Of course they did not realize how difficult and perplexing they were making the examinations for me. How could they—they can see and hear, and I suppose they could not understand matters from my point of view. . . .

Thus far my summer has been sweeter than anything I can remember. My mother, and sister and little brother have been here five weeks, and our happiness knows no bounds. Not only do we enjoy being together; but we also find our little home most delightful. I do wish you could see the view of the beautiful lake from our piazza, the islands looking like little emerald peaks in the golden sunlight, and the canoes flitting here and there, like autumn leaves in the gentle breeze, and breathe in the peculiarly delicious fragrance of the woods, which comes like a murmur from an unknown clime. I cannot help wondering if it is the same fragrance that greeted the Norsemen long ago, when, according to tradition, they visited our shores—an odorous echo of many centuries of silent growth and decay in flower and tree. . . .

TO MRS. SAMUEL RICHARD FULLER

Wrentham, October 20, 1899.

. . . I suppose it is time for me to tell you something about our plans for the winter. You know it has long been my ambition to go to Radcliffe, and receive a degree, as many other girls have done, but Dean Irwin of Radcliffe, has persuaded me to take a special course for the present. She said I had already shown the world that I could do the college work, by passing all my examinations successfully, in spite of many obstacles. She showed me how very foolish it would be for me to pursue a four years' course of study at Radcliffe, simply to be like other girls, when I might better be cultivating whatever ability I had for writing. She said she did not consider a degree of any real value, but

thought it was much more desirable to do something
original than to waste one's energies only for a degree.
Her arguments seemed so wise and practical, that I
could not but yield. I found it hard, very hard, to give
up the idea of going to college; it had been in my mind
ever since I was a little girl; but there is no use doing a
foolish thing, because one has wanted to do it a long
time, is there?

But, while we were discussing plans for the winter,
a suggestion which Dr. Hale had made long ago
flashed across Teacher's mind—that I might take
courses somewhat like those offered at Radcliffe,
under the instruction of the professors in those courses.
Miss Irwin seemed to have no objection to this
proposal, and kindly offered to see the professors and
find out if they would give me lessons. If they will be
so good as to teach me and if we have money enough
to do as we have planned, my studies this year will be
English, English Literature of the Elizabethan period,
Latin and German....

TO MR. JOHN HITZ

138 Brattle St., Cambridge,
Nov. 11, 1899.

... As to the braille question, I cannot tell how deeply
it distresses me to hear that my statement with regard
to the examinations has been doubted. Ignorance
seems to be at the bottom of all those contradictions.
Why, you yourself seem to think that I taught you
American braille, when you do not know a single
letter in the system! I could not help laughing when
you said you had been writing to me in American
braille—and there you were writing your letter in
English braille!

The facts about the braille examinations are as
follows:

How I passed my Entrance Examinations
for Radcliffe College.

On the 29th and 30th of June, 1899, I took my
examinations for Radcliffe College. The first day I had
elementary Greek and advanced Latin, and the second
day Geometry, Algebra and advanced Greek.

The college authorities would not permit Miss
Sullivan to read the examination papers to me; so Mr.
Eugene C. Vining, one of the instructors at the Perkins
Institution for the Blind, was employed to copy the
papers for me in braille. Mr. Vining was a perfect
stranger to me, and could not communicate with me
except by writing in braille. The Proctor also was a
stranger, and did not attempt to communicate with me
in any way; and, as they were both unfamiliar with my
speech, they could not readily understand what I said
to them.

However, the braille worked well enough in the
languages; but when it came to Geometry and
Algebra, it was quite different. I was sorely perplexed,
and felt quite discouraged, and wasted much precious
time, especially in Algebra. It is true that I am
perfectly familiar with all literary braille—English,
American and New York Point; but the method of
writing the various signs used in Geometry and
Algebra in the three systems is very different, and two
days before the examinations I knew only the English
method. I had used it all through my school work, and
never any other system.

In Geometry, my chief difficulty was, that I had
always been accustomed to reading the propositions in
Line Print, or having them spelled into my hand; and
somehow, although the propositions were right before
me, yet the braille confused me, and I could not fix in
my mind clearly what I was reading. But, when I took
up Algebra, I had a harder time still—I was terribly
handicapped by my imperfect knowledge of the

notation. The signs, which I had learned the day before, and which I thought I knew perfectly, confused me. Consequently my work was painfully slow, and I was obliged to read the examples over and over before I could form a clear idea what I was required to do. Indeed, I am not sure now that I read all the signs correctly, especially as I was much distressed, and found it very hard to keep my wits about me. . . .

Now there is one more fact, which I wish to state very plainly, in regard to what Mr. Gilman wrote to you. I never received any direct instruction in the Gilman School. Miss Sullivan always sat beside me, and told me what the teachers said. I did teach Miss Hall, my teacher in Physics, how to write the American braille, but she never gave me any instruction by means of it, unless a few problems written for practice, which made me waste much precious time deciphering them, can be called instruction. Dear Frau Gröte learned the manual alphabet, and used to teach me herself; but this was in private lessons, which were paid for by my friends. In the German class Miss Sullivan interpreted to me as well as she could what the teacher said.

Perhaps, if you would send a copy of this to the head of the Cambridge School, it might enlighten his mind on a few subjects, on which he seems to be in total darkness just now. . . .

TO MISS MILDRED KELLER

138 Brattle Street, Cambridge,
November 26, 1899.

. . . At last we are settled for the winter, and our work is going smoothly. Mr. Keith comes every afternoon at four o'clock, and gives me a "friendly lift" over the rough stretches of road, over which every student must go. I am studying English history, English literature, French and Latin, and by and by I shall take up German and English composition—let us groan! You know, I detest grammar as much as you do; but I suppose I must go through it if I am to write, just as we had to get ducked in the lake hundreds of times before we could swim! In French Teacher is reading "Columbia" to me. It is a delightful novel, full of piquant expressions and thrilling adventures (don't dare to blame me for using big words, since you do the same!) and, if you ever read it, I think you will enjoy it immensely. You are studying English history, aren't you? O but it's exceedingly interesting! I'm making quite a thorough study of the Elizabethan period—of the Reformation, and the Acts of Supremacy and Conformity, and the maritime discoveries, and all the big things, which the "deuce" seems to have invented to plague innocent youngsters like yourself! . . .

Now we have a swell winter outfit—coats, hats, gowns, flannels and all. We've just had four lovely dresses made by a French dressmaker. I have two, of which one has a black silk skirt, with a black lace net over it, and a waist of white poplin, with turquoise velvet and chiffon, and cream lace over a satin yoke. The other is woollen, and of a very pretty green. The waist is trimmed with pink and green brocaded velvet, and white lace, I think, and has double reefers on the front, tucked and trimmed with velvet, and also a row of tiny white buttons. Teacher too has a silk dress. The skirt is black, while the waist is mostly yellow, trimmed with delicate lavender chiffon, and black velvet bows and lace. Her other dress is purple, trimmed with purple velvet, and the waist has a collar of cream lace. So you may imagine that we look quite like peacocks, only we've no trains. . . .

A week ago yesterday there was [a] great football game between Harvard and Yale, and there was tremendous excitement here. We could hear the yells

of the boys and the cheers of the lookers-on as plainly
in our room as if we had been on the field. Colonel
Roosevelt was there, on Harvard's side; but bless you,
he wore a white sweater, and no crimson that we know
of! There were about twenty-five thousand people at
the game, and when we went out, the noise was so
terrific, we nearly jumped out of our skins, thinking it
was the din of war, and not a football game that we
heard. But, in spite of all their wild efforts, neither side
was scored, and we all laughed and said, "Oh, well,
now the pot can't call the kettle black!"...

TO MRS. LAURENCE HUTTON

559 Madison Avenue, New York,
January 2, 1900.

...We have been here a week now, and are going to
stay with Miss Rhoades until Saturday. We are
enjoying every moment of our visit, every one is so
good to us. We have seen many of our old friends, and
made some new ones. We dined with the Rogers last
Friday, and oh, they were so kind to us! The thought of
their gentle courtesy and genuine kindness brings a
warm glow of joy and gratitude to my heart. I have
seen Dr. Greer too. He has such a kind heart! I love
him more than ever. We went to St. Bartholomew's
Sunday, and I have not felt so much at home in a
church since dear Bishop Brooks died. Dr. Greer read
so slowly, that my teacher could tell me every word.
His people must have wondered at his unusual
deliberation. After the service he asked Mr. Warren,
the organist to play for me. I stood in the middle of the
church, where the vibrations from the great organ were
strongest, and I felt the mighty waves of sound beat
against me, as the great billows beat against a little
ship at sea.

TO MR. JOHN HITZ

138 Brattle Street, Cambridge,
Feb. 3, 1900.

... My studies are more interesting than ever. In Latin, I am reading Horace's odes. Although I find them difficult to translate, yet I think they are the loveliest pieces of Latin poetry I have read or shall ever read. In French we have finished "Colomba," and I am reading "Horace" by Corneille and La Fontaine's fables, both of which are in braille. I have not gone far in either; but I know I shall enjoy the fables, they are so delightfully written, and give such good lessons in a simple and yet attractive way. I do not think I have told you that my dear teacher is reading "The Faery Queen" to me. I am afraid I find fault with the poem as much as I enjoy it. I do not care much for the allegories, indeed I often find them tiresome, and I cannot help thinking that Spenser's world of knights, paynims, fairies, dragons and all sorts of strange creatures is a somewhat grotesque and amusing world; but the poem itself is lovely and as musical as a running brook.

I am now the proud owner of about fifteen new books, which we ordered from Louisville. Among them are "Henry Esmond," "Bacon's Essays" and extracts from "English Literature." Perhaps next week I shall have some more books, "The Tempest," "A Midsummer Night's Dream" and possibly some selections from Green's history of England. Am I not very fortunate?

I am afraid this letter savors too much of books— but really they make up my whole life these days, and I scarcely see or hear of anything else! I do believe I sleep on books every night! You know a student's life is of necessity somewhat circumscribed and narrow and crowds out almost everything that is not in books....

TO THE CHAIRMAN OF THE ACADEMIC BOARD
OF RADCLIFFE COLLEGE

138 Brattle Street, Cambridge, Mass.,
May 5, 1900.

Dear Sir:

As an aid to me in determining my plans for study the coming year, I apply to you for information as to the possibility of my taking the regular courses in Radcliffe College.

Since receiving my certificate of admission to Radcliffe last July, I have been studying with a private tutor, Horace, Aeschylus, French, German, Rhetoric, English History, English Literature and Criticism, and English composition.

In college I should wish to continue most, if not all of these subjects. The conditions under which I work require the presence of Miss Sullivan, who has been my teacher and companion for thirteen years, as an interpreter of oral speech and as a reader of examination papers. In college she, or possibly in some subjects some one else, would of necessity be with me in the lecture-room and at recitations. I should do all my written work on a typewriter, and if a Professor could not understand my speech, I could write out my answers to his questions and hand them to him after the recitation.

Is it possible for the College to accommodate itself to these unprecedented conditions, so as to enable me to pursue my studies at Radcliffe? I realize that the obstacles in the way of my receiving a college education are very great—to others they may seem insurmountable; but, dear Sir, a true soldier does not acknowledge defeat before the battle.

TO MRS. LAURENCE HUTTON

138 Brattle Street, Cambridge,
June 9, 1900.

... I have not yet heard from the Academic Board in reply to my letter; but I sincerely hope they will answer favorably. My friends think it very strange that they should hesitate so long, especially when I have not asked them to simplify my work in the least, but only to modify it so as to meet the existing circumstances. Cornell has offered to make arrangements suited to the conditions under which I work, if I should decide to go to that college, and the University of Chicago has made a similar offer; but I am afraid if I went to any other college, it would be thought that I did not pass my examinations for Radcliffe satisfactorily. ...

In the fall Miss Keller entered Radcliffe College.

TO MR. JOHN HITZ

14 Coolidge Ave., Cambridge,
Nov. 26, 1900.

... —— has already communicated with you in regard to her and my plan of establishing an institution for deaf and blind children. At first I was most enthusiastic in its support, and I never dreamed that any grave objections could be raised except indeed by those who are hostile to Teacher; but now, after thinking most *seriously* and consulting my friends, I have decided that ——'s plan is by no means feasible. In my eagerness to make it possible for deaf and blind children to have the same advantages that I have had, I quite forgot that there might be many obstacles in the way of my accomplishing anything like what —— proposed.

My friends thought we might have one or two pupils in our own home, thereby securing to me the advantage of being helpful to others without any of the disadvantages of a large school. They were very kind; but I could not help feeling that they spoke more from a business than a humanitarian point of view. I am sure they did not quite understand how passionately I desire that all who are afflicted like myself shall receive their rightful inheritance of thought, knowledge and love. Still I could not shut my eyes to the force and weight of their arguments, and I saw plainly that I must abandon ——'s scheme as impracticable. They also said that I ought to appoint an advisory committee to control my affairs while I am at Radcliffe. I considered this suggestion carefully, then I told Mr. Rhoades that I should be proud and glad to have wise friends to whom I could always turn for advice in all important matters. For this committee I chose six, my mother, Teacher, because she is like a mother to me, Mrs. Hutton, Mr. Rhoades, Dr. Greer and Mr. Rogers, because it is they who have supported me all these years and made it possible for me to enter college. Mrs. Hutton had already written to mother, asking her to telegraph if she was willing for me to have other advisers besides herself and Teacher. This morning we received word that mother had given her consent to this arrangement. Now it remains for me to write to Dr. Greer and Mr. Rogers. . . .

We had a long talk with Dr. Bell. Finally he proposed a plan which delighted us all beyond words. He said that it was a gigantic blunder to attempt to found a school for deaf and blind children, because then they would lose the most precious opportunities of entering into the fuller, richer, freer life of seeing and hearing children. I had had misgivings on this point; but I could not see how we were to help it. However Mr. Bell suggested that —— and all her

friends who are interested in her scheme should
organize an association for the promotion of the
education of the deaf and blind, Teacher and myself
being included, of course. Under his plan they were
to appoint Teacher to train others to instruct deaf
and blind children in their own homes, just as she
had taught me. Funds were to be raised for the
teachers' lodgings and also for their salaries. At the
same time Dr. Bell added that I could rest content
and fight my way through Radcliffe in competition
with seeing and hearing girls, while the great desire
of my heart was being fulfilled. We clapped our
hands and shouted; —— went away beaming with
pleasure, and Teacher and I felt more light of heart
than we had for sometime. Of course we can do
nothing just now; but the painful anxiety about my
college work and the future welfare of the deaf and
blind has been lifted from our minds. Do tell me
what you think about Dr. Bell's suggestion. It seems
most practical and wise to me; but I must know all
that there is to be known about it before I speak or act
in the matter....

TO MR. JOHN D. WRIGHT

Cambridge, December 9, 1900.
Do you think me a villain and—I can't think of a word
bad enough to express your opinion of me, unless
indeed horse-thief will answer the purpose. Tell me
truly, do you think me as bad as that? I hope not; for
I have thought many letters to you which never got
on paper, and I am delighted to get your good letter,
yes, I really was, and I intended to answer it
immediately; but the days slip by unnoticed when one
is busy, and I have been very busy this fall. You must
believe that. Radcliffe girls are always up to their ears

in work. If you doubt it, you'd better come and see for
yourself.

Yes, I am taking the regular college course for a
degree. When I am a B.A., I suppose you will not dare
call me a villain! I am studying English—Sophomore
English, if you please, (though I can't see that it is
different from just plain English) German, French and
History. I'm enjoying my work even more than I
expected to, which is another way of saying that I'm
glad I came. It is hard, very hard at times; but it hasn't
swamped me yet. No, I am not studying Mathematics,
or Greek or Latin either. The courses at Radcliffe are
elective, only certain courses in English are
prescribed. I passed off my English and advanced
French before I entered college, and I choose the
courses I like best. I don't however intend to give up
Latin and Greek entirely. Perhaps I shall take up these
studies later; but I've said goodbye to Mathematics
forever, and I assure you, I was delighted to see the
last of those horrid goblins! I hope to obtain my
degree in four years; but I'm not very particular about
that. There's no great hurry, and I want to get as much
as possible out of my studies. Many of my friends
would be well pleased if I would take two or even one
course a year; but I rather object to spending the rest
of my life in college. . . .

TO MR. WILLIAM WADE

*14 Coolidge Avenue, Cambridge,
December 9, 1900.*

. . . Since you are so much interested in the deaf and
blind, I will begin by telling you of several cases I
have come across lately. Last October I heard of an
unusually bright little girl in Texas. Her name is Ruby
Rice, and she is thirteen years old, I think. She has
never been taught; but they say she can sew and likes

to help others in this sort of work. Her sense of smell
is wonderful. Why, when she enters a store, she will
go straight to the showcases, and she can also
distinguish her own things. Her parents are very
anxious indeed to find a teacher for her. They have
also written to Mr. Hitz about her.

I also know a child at the Institution for the Deaf
in Mississippi. Her name is Maud Scott, and she is
six years old. Miss Watkins, the lady who has charge
of her wrote me a most interesting letter. She said
that Maud was born deaf and lost her sight when she
was only three months old, and that when she went
to the Institution a few weeks ago, she was quite
helpless. She could not even walk and had very little
use of her hands. When they tried to teach her to
string beads, her little hands fell to her side.
Evidently her sense of touch has not been developed,
and as yet she can walk only when she holds some
one's hand; but she seems to be an exceedingly bright
child. Miss Watkins adds that she is very pretty. I have
written to her that when Maud learns to read, I shall
have many stories to send her. The dear, sweet little
girl, it makes my heart ache to think how utterly she is
cut off from all that is good and desirable in life. But
Miss Watkins seems to be just the kind of teacher she
needs.

I was in New York not long ago and I saw Miss
Rhoades, who told me that she had seen Katie McGirr.
She said the poor young girl talked and acted exactly
like a little child. Katie played with Miss Rhoades's
rings and took them away, saying with a merry laugh,
"You shall not have them again!" She could only
understand Miss Rhoades when she talked about the
simplest things. The latter wished to send her some
books; but she could not find anything simple enough
for her! She said Katie was very sweet indeed, but
sadly in need of proper instruction. I was much

surprised to hear all this; for I judged from your letters that Katie was a very precocious girl....

A few days ago I met Tommy Stringer in the railroad station at Wrentham. He is a great, strong boy now, and he will soon need a man to take care of him; he is really too big for a lady to manage. He goes to the public school, I hear, and his progress is astonishing, they say; but it doesn't show as yet in his conversation, which is limited to "Yes" and "No." ...

TO MR. CHARLES T. COPELAND

December 20, 1900.

My dear Mr. Copeland:

I venture to write to you because I am afraid that if I do not explain why I have stopped writing themes, you will think I have become discouraged, or perhaps that to escape criticism I have beat a cowardly retreat from your class. Please do not think either of these very unpleasant thoughts. I am not discouraged, nor am I afraid. I am confident that I could go on writing themes like those I have written, and I suppose I should get through the course with fairly good marks; but this sort of literary patchwork has lost all interest for me. I have never been satisfied with my work; but I never knew what my difficulty was until you pointed it out to me. When I came to your class last October, I was trying with all my might to be like everybody else, to forget as entirely as possible my limitations and peculiar environment. Now, however, I see the folly of attempting to hitch one's wagon to a star with harness that does not belong to it.

I have always accepted other people's experiences and observations as a matter of course. It never occurred to me that it might be worth while to make my own observations and describe the experiences peculiarly my own. Henceforth I am resolved to be myself, to live my own life and write my own thoughts when I have any. When I have written something that seems to be fresh and spontaneous and worthy of your criticisms, I will bring it to you, if I may, and if you think it good, I shall be happy; but if your verdict is unfavorable, I shall try again and yet again until I have succeeded in pleasing you. . . .

TO MRS. LAURENCE HUTTON

14 Coolidge Avenue, Cambridge,
December 27, 1900.

. . . So you read about our class luncheon in the papers? How in the world do the papers find out everything, I wonder. I am sure no reporter was present. I had a splendid time; the toasts and speeches were great fun. I only spoke a few words, as I did not know I was expected to speak until a few minutes before I was called upon. I think I wrote you that I had been elected Vice-President of the Freshman Class of Radcliffe.

Did I tell you in my last letter that I had a new dress, a real party dress with low neck and short sleeves and quite a train? It is pale blue, trimmed with chiffon of the same color. I have worn it only once, but then I felt that Solomon in all his glory was not to be compared with me! Anyway, he certainly never had a dress like mine! . . .

A gentleman in Philadelphia has just written to my teacher about a deaf and blind child in Paris, whose parents are Poles. The mother is a physician and a brilliant woman, he says. This little boy could speak two or three languages before he lost his hearing through sickness, and he is now only about five years old. Poor little fellow, I wish I could do something for him; but he is so young, my teacher thinks it would be too bad to separate him from his mother. I have had a

letter from Mrs. Thaw with regard to the possibility of
doing something for these children. Dr. Bell thinks the
present census will show that there are more than a
thousand in the United States alone; and Mrs. Thaw
thinks if all my friends were to unite their efforts, "it
would be an easy matter to establish at the beginning
of this new century a new line upon which mercy
might travel," and the rescue of those unfortunate
children could be accomplished....

TO MR. WILLIAM WADE

Cambridge, February 2, 1901.

... By the way, have you any specimens of English
braille especially printed for those who have lost their
sight late in life or have fingers hardened by long toil,
so that their touch is less sensitive than that of other
blind people? I read an account of such a system in one
of my English magazines, and I am anxious to know
more about it. If it is as efficient as they say, I see no
reason why English braille should not be adopted by
the blind of all countries. Why, it is the print that can
be most readily adapted to many different languages.
Even Greek can be embossed in it, as you know. Then,
too, it will be rendered still more efficient by the
"interpointing system" which will save an immense
amount of space and paper. There is nothing more
absurd, I think, than to have five or six different prints
for the blind....

This letter was written in response to a tentative offer from the
editor of *The Great Round World* to have the magazine published in raised type for the blind, if enough were willing to
subscribe. It is evident that the blind should have a good magazine, not a special magazine for the blind, but one of our best
monthlies, printed in embossed letters. The blind alone could

not support it, but it would not take very much money to make up the additional expense.

TO *The Great Round World*

Cambridge, Feb. 16, 1901.

The Great Round World,
New York City.
Gentlemen: I have only to-day found time to reply to your interesting letter. A little bird had already sung the good news in my ear; but it was doubly pleasant to have it straight from you.

It would be splendid to have *The Great Round World* printed in "language that can be felt." I doubt if any one who enjoys the wondrous privilege of seeing can have any conception of the boon such a publication as you contemplate would be to the sightless. To be able to read for one's self what is being willed, thought and done in the world—the world in whose joys and sorrows, failures and successes one feels the keenest interest—that would indeed be a happiness too deep for words. I trust that the effort of *The Great Round World* to bring light to those who sit in darkness will receive the encouragement and support it so richly deserves.

I doubt, however, if the number of subscribers to an embossed edition of *The Great Round World* would ever be large; for I am told that the blind as a class are poor. But why should not the friends of the blind assist *The Great Round World*, if necessary? Surely there are hearts and hands ever ready to make it possible for generous intentions to be wrought into noble deeds.

Wishing you godspeed in an undertaking that is very dear to my heart, I am, etc.

TO MISS NINA RHOADES

Cambridge, Sept. 25, 1901.

... We remained in Halifax until about the middle of August.... Day after day the Harbor, the warships, and the park kept us busy thinking and feeling and enjoying.... When the *Indiana* visited Halifax, we were invited to go on board, and she sent her own launch for us. I touched the immense cannon, read with my fingers several of the names of the Spanish ships that were captured at Santiago, and felt the places where she had been pierced with shells. The *Indiana* was the largest and finest ship in the Harbor, and we felt very proud of her.

After we left Halifax, we visited Dr. Bell at Cape Breton. He has a charming, romantic house on a mountain called Beinn Bhreagh, which overlooks the Bras d'Or Lake....

Dr. Bell told me many interesting things about his work. He had just constructed a boat that could be propelled by a kite with the wind in its favor, and one day he tried experiments to see if he could steer the kite against the wind. I was there and really helped him fly the kites. On one of them I noticed that the strings were of wire, and having had some experience in bead work, I said I thought they would break. Dr. Bell said "No!" with great confidence, and the kite was sent up. It began to pull and tug, and lo, the wires broke, and off went the great red dragon, and poor Dr. Bell stood looking forlornly after it. After that he asked me if the strings were all right and changed them at once when I answered in the negative. Altogether we had great fun....

TO DR. EDWARD EVERETT HALE*

Cambridge, Nov. 10, 1901.

My teacher and I expect to be present at the meeting tomorrow in commemoration of the one hundredth anniversary of Dr. Howe's birth; but I very much doubt if we shall have an opportunity to speak with you; so I am writing now to tell you how delighted I am that you are to speak at the meeting, because I feel that you, better than any one I know will express the heartfelt gratitude of those who owe their education, their opportunities, their happiness to him who opened the eyes of the blind and gave the dumb lip language.

Sitting here in my study, surrounded by my books, enjoying the sweet and intimate companionship of the great and the wise, I am trying to realize what my life might have been, if Dr. Howe had failed in the great task God gave him to perform. If he had not taken upon himself the responsibility of Laura Bridgman's education and led her out of the pit of Acheron back to her human inheritance, should I be a sophomore at Radcliffe College today—who can say? But it is idle to speculate about what might have been in connection with Dr. Howe's great achievement.

I think only those who have escaped that death-in-life existence, from which Laura Bridgman was rescued, can realize how isolated, how shrouded in darkness, how cramped by its own impotence is a soul without thought or faith or hope. Words are powerless to describe the desolation of that prison-house, or the joy of the soul that is delivered out of its captivity. When we compare the needs and helplessness of the

---

*Read by Dr. Hale at the celebration of the centenary of Dr. Samuel Gridley Howe, at Tremont Temple, Boston, Nov. 11, 1901.

blind before Dr. Howe began his work, with their
present usefulness and independence, we realize that
great things have been done in our midst. What if
physical conditions have built up high walls about
us? Thanks to our friend and helper, our world lies
upward; the length and breadth and sweep of the
heavens are ours!

It is pleasant to think that Dr. Howe's noble deeds
will receive their due tribute of affection and
gratitude, in the city, which was the scene of his great
labors and splendid victories for humanity.

With kind greetings, in which my teacher joins me,
I am

> Affectionately your friend,
> HELEN A. KELLER

TO THE HON. GEORGE FRISBIE HOAR

> *Cambridge, Mass., November 25, 1901.*

My Dear Senator Hoar:—

I am glad you liked my letter about Dr. Howe. It was
written out of my heart, and perhaps that is why it met
a sympathetic response in other hearts. I will ask Dr.
Hale to lend me the letter, so that I can make a copy of
it for you.

You see, I use a typewriter—it is my right hand
man, so to speak. Without it I do not see how I could
go to college. I write all my themes and examinations
on it, even Greek. Indeed, it has only one drawback,
and that probably is regarded as an advantage by the
professors; it is that one's mistakes may be detected at
a glance; for there is no chance to hide them in
illegible writing.

I know you will be amused when I tell you that I
am deeply interested in politics. I like to have the
papers read to me, and I try to understand the great

questions of the day; but I am afraid my knowledge is very unstable; for I change my opinions with every new book I read. I used to think that when I studied Civil Government and Economics, all my difficulties and perplexities would blossom into beautiful certainties; but alas, I find that there are more tares than wheat in these fertile fields of knowledge. . . .

SEE YOUR BOOKSELLER FOR THESE
BANTAM CLASSICS

THE AWAKENING, Kate Chopin, 0-553-21330-X
THE WOMAN IN WHITE, Wilkie Collins, 0-553-21263-X
HEART OF DARKNESS and THE SECRET SHARER, Joseph Conrad, 0-553-21214-1
LORD JIM, Joseph Conrad, 0-553-21361-X
THE DEERSLAYER, James Fenimore Cooper, 0-553-21085-8
THE LAST OF THE MOHICANS, James Fenimore Cooper, 0-553-21329-6
MAGGIE: A GIRL OF THE STREETS AND OTHER SHORT FICTION, Stephen Crane, 0-553-21355-5
THE RED BADGE OF COURAGE, Stephen Crane, 0-553-21011-4
THE INFERNO, Dante, 0-553-21339-3
PARADISO, Dante, 0-553-21204-4
PURGATORIO, Dante, 0-553-21344-X
THE ORIGIN OF SPECIES, Charles Darwin, 0-553-21463-2
MOLL FLANDERS, Daniel Defoe, 0-553-21328-8
ROBINSON CRUSOE, Daniel Defoe, 0-553-21373-3
BLEAK HOUSE, Charles Dickens, 0-553-21223-0
A CHRISTMAS CAROL, Charles Dickens, 0-553-21244-3
DAVID COPPERFIELD, Charles Dickens, 0-553-21189-7
GREAT EXPECTATIONS, Charles Dickens, 0-553-21342-3
HARD TIMES, Charles Dickens, 0-553-21016-5
OLIVER TWIST, Charles Dickens, 0-553-21102-1
THE PICKWICK PAPERS, Charles Dickens, 0-553-21123-4
A TALE OF TWO CITIES, Charles Dickens, 0-553-21176-5
THREE SOLDIERS, John Dos Passos, 0-553-21456-X
THE BROTHERS KARAMAZOV, Fyodor Dostoevsky, 0-553-21216-8
CRIME AND PUNISHMENT, Fyodor Dostoevsky, 0-553-21175-7
THE ETERNAL HUSBAND AND OTHER STORIES, Fyodor Dostoevsky, 0-553-21444-6
THE IDIOT, Fyodor Dostoevsky, 0-553-21352-0
NOTES FROM UNDERGROUND, Fyodor Dostoevsky, 0-553-21144-7
SHERLOCK HOLMES VOL I, Sir Arthur Conan Doyle, 0-553-21241-9
SHERLOCK HOLMES VOL II, Sir Arthur Conan Doyle, 0-553-21242-7
SISTER CARRIE, Theodore Dreiser, 0-553-21374-1
THE SOULS OF BLACK FOLK, W. E. B. Du Bois, 0-553-21336-9
THE COUNT OF MONTE CRISTO, Alexandre Dumas, 0-553-21350-4
THE THREE MUSKETEERS, Alexandre Dumas, 0-553-21337-7
MIDDLEMARCH, George Eliot, 0-553-21180-3
SILAS MARNER, George Eliot, 0-553-21229-X

THE PICTURE OF DORIAN GRAY AND OTHER WRITINGS, Oscar Wilde, 0-553-21254-0

THE SWISS FAMILY ROBINSON, Johann David Wyss, 0-553-21403-9

EARLY AFRICAN-AMERICAN CLASSICS, 0-553-21379-2

FIFTY GREAT SHORT STORIES, 0-553-27745-6

FIFTY GREAT AMERICAN SHORT STORIES, 0-553-27294-2

SHORT SHORTS, 0-553-27440-6